Some bedtime reading
with love from Joe

Observations

by the same author

KITCHEN IN THE CORNER
ROUNDABOUT
ONLY ON SUNDAYS
WHITEHORN'S SOCIAL SURVIVAL

Observations

KATHARINE WHITEHORN

METHUEN & CO LTD

11 NEW FETTER LANE LONDON EC4

First published in 1970 by Methuen & Co Ltd,
11 New Fetter Lane, London EC4
© *The Observer 1967, 1968, 1969, 1970*
Printed in Great Britain by
Latimer Trend & Co Ltd Plymouth

SBN 416 08210 6

With love and thanks to
my parents who provide so much copy

Acknowledgments

My thanks are due to the editor of the *Observer*, in which these articles first appeared.

K.W.

Contents

1 · *The Disgusting Side of Gardening*

There used to be a character on *Picture Post* for whom we all felt an affectionate pity. Every time we were racked by some crisis such as Suez or a cut in our expenses or one of our twice-monthly changes of editor, and the rest of us were all racing about with blazing eyes discussing the awfulness of it all, he would say: 'Well – I'd better get back to my cabbages.' And off he would go to darkest Bucks with the serenity of the beautiful people.

Now that I am in the early stages of his very malady, I begin to understand him better – and I'm inclined to think the flower-hung beautiful people are not all they seem, either. They aren't drug addicts; they're gardeners.

I am not yet a real gardener. I define a real gardener as the man who stands beaming over one wretched little blue flower the size of your fingernail saying: 'Look at that! And for four years it never did a thing!' But I have passed several of the milestones of decline, and I fear that even that sort of patience may not be so very far off.

The first is the point at which you note with surprise that you cannot lie contentedly on the lawn entirely surrounded by your own weeds. The second is where you refuse to take flowers for the house because you want to leave them in the garden; the third (O noble rot) is compost. I've no doubt compost will turn out to be a damp squib like all my other cure-alls, but it at least bodes the sort of hope you can smell all the way down the garden.

And hope, it must be admitted, is vital to this gardening business. Next year, you say, as you lean back with the Planter's Handbook, it will all be different. I will remember where I have put things and not have so many a flower born to blush unseen because I've planted it behind a peony; next year I will arrange it so that the few things that *do* come up are not all in different and quarrelling shades of red; next year I will not allow a keen helper to weed up the forget-me-not in a fit of absence of mind.

Every year you assure yourself that next year you will remember what you have learnt this year. And, in fact, I have learnt a bit, with all these trials. I now realize that seeds, which seem so easy, are difficult, but that if you buy things actually in flower it is probably too late to get the best out of them: little plants with a sturdy background seem best. I've learned that for practical purposes perennials are the ones that grow like weeds, biennials are the ones that die this year instead of next and hardy annuals are the ones that never come up at all.

I'm learning that if your soil is composed in equal parts of clay and catdirt things are just not going to spread and burgeon as if in country loam, and that though the long-term answer is endless soil enrichment, the short-term one is to buy twice as many plants as you'd otherwise need. And I have learned enough to ensure that next year I shall not have to relive the moment when I gestured towards one of the few plants that really was doing quite well, and my father took me gently by the hand and said: 'It is a weed.'

What I had never realized, before I got hooked on this thing, was how much of the pleasure of gardening is purely destructive. Poetesses may talk with fervour about nurturing young green lives, but what one really gets a kick out of is hacking back old brown ones, gouging huge holes out of the earth, hauling out weeds by the roots. And as for pruning

. . . I walk stiffly away from pruning, my bloodstained secateurs in hand, with the zombie-like look of a Hitchcock villain who knows he has Gone Too Far.

Even advanced gardeners, I believe, spend half their life dreaming of extermination – of death to pests and skulduggery to the slugs. Why, my pacific father once sent me a postcard which read SLUG DEATH SLAYS THOUSANDS TERRIBLE HOLOCAUST IN WILTSHIRE GARDEN. Getting rid of plants you hate is almost as rewarding (and a lot easier) than rearing the ones you like; and friends who give you boxes of unidentified cuttings ensure a plentiful supply of these. Even the ones who kindly label things like 'dahlia – yellow – 18 inches high' always include a few unlabelled surprises – like 'worm, pink, three feet long'.

Worms aside, I confess I get a great charge out of the disgusting side of gardening. I cannot yet claim, like the man in the anecdote, that my stench is as the stench of ten because I cart manure – not being inclined to run through the streets shouting 'A horse, a horse, my column for a horse' I don't see how I can get any; and the only time a man came with some to sell was on a day I was expecting ten infants to tea in the garden.

Nor do I have the dedication of a relation by marriage who used to be seen in his dressing-gown through the morning mists bearing a steaming jerry to his marrows: 'diluted, of course,' he would say severely.

But just listen to this from C. E. Lucas Phillips's *The Small Garden*: 'The stuff that can go into the heap comprises the vegetable matter from flower or kitchen garden, hedgerow or common, especially nettles . . . household refuse such as eggshells, fruit and vegetable peelings, fish waste, vacuum cleaner contents, tealeaves; the dung of horse, cow, pig, chicken, etc.' For sheer squelch, it's better than Whiffle on the Pig, Lord Emsworth's favourite reading.

Reading about it, of course, is not the same as doing it. But either way, your viewpoint completely alters. I've started to like rain, just as my father has begun to hate birds: 'Nasty little birds: eat my polyanthus,' he says – and ties up black thread which they can't see to trip them up as they swoop in to the attack. The only trouble is he can't see it either, and performs a sort of eurythmic cats' cradle as he wrestles with an invisible foe.

And I think I begin to understand, through a garden smaller than a tennis court, a little of what it is that makes stockbrokers sell their souls to become farmers. It is all quite frightful: everything in sight has the bots, the staggers, wireworm and the pip; it hasn't rained, it hasn't been sunny; there is moss in the lawn, cats in the catmint, the sheep's in the meadow, the cow's in corn.

And yet nothing fills you up so completely with the clear, cool wash of contentment, like a jug of muddy water washed clean. Excuse me: I have to go and activate the compost.

2 · Getting Over a Bad Case of the Builders

In the days when one hung from a picture hook by the teeth grappling a damp piece of wallpaper in one's outstretched arms, the idea of getting a man to do it all seemed like El Dorado. Now, after two years of their more or less constant company, I answer anyone who says 'I've got the builders' with the same appalled sympathy as if they'd said 'I've got the shingles'.

Builders walk painty feet across the carpets, builders don't turn up when you expect them, builders get milk from a different milkman from yours and leave the bottles littering the doorstep for months. Many of them are personally charming: we had a nice Jamaican who used to drink rum with my husband after hours and complain about unseasoned British timber; a saintlike carpenter foreman who used to encourage us by saying: 'To men of our calibre all things are possible' and enrage us by saying: 'Everything comes to him who waits.'

One painter was so good with the children it took us days to realize he wasn't actually doing any painting to speak of; we almost advertised for 'Nanny – experienced housepainter' to right the domestic balance. They all seemed happy to spend the rest of their lives with us; and the quiet now they've gone is wonderful; but we have learned a few things from our mistakes.

An old house is a mistake, if you want to stay solvent: there is no good stopping place, and you could well go on until you'd rebuilt it completely. We kept on running out of money or ideas or stamina and calling a halt – which is like having one tooth filled every Tuesday for months instead of getting it all over in one grim morning. And on one of our three bouts we were fool enough to try to handle things ourselves instead of getting in an umpire or middle man.

These are invaluable, for two reasons. First, because you have someone powerful gunning for you when things go wrong; secondly, because they can see the consequences of what you want – doors that will have to be re-hung if you put up that shelf, walls that will fall down if you knock through too big a hole.

Such a middle man will also know the difference between one builder and another – and they vary enormously. The root trouble of the building trade is lack of skilled labour, which leads to lack of discipline – if the boss complains about their tea breaks they go elsewhere; to unreliability, because half the time the work force has knocked off to do a private job on the side for which it is paid in greasy tax-free notes; and to the proliferation of little firms – a plumber and a carpenter setting up shop with a couple of mates so as not to let the boss get all the money.

Further delays are caused by the time everything takes to deliver – especially if it hasn't been ordered yet: it's worth nagging to make sure that orders for wallpapers, laminated hardboard, appliances really have been put in at the beginning.

And there are other delays which are just like the delays of do-it-yourself: you only need one job to be a bit more awkward than it looked, a couple of screws to break off on meeting unsuspected concrete and a bit of paint to take an extra half-hour to dry and you're hours behind. Which is why the only way to stay calm is just to resign yourself to every job taking twice as long as you expect. I know someone who drives through the London rush hour every day in complete calm: 'by not hoping it will take less time than I know it always does,' she says. That's the attitude.

It's not only time you have to allow twice as much of as you thought: it's money. It's true that some builders estimate low to get the job and then slap on the extras; but mostly they hardly have to kid us because we're so busy kidding ourselves – making believe we can have the House Beautiful for twenty quid.

Half the heartbreak in the building situation is the result of misunderstanding – and the more pleasant the chap, the more likely you are to think you've communicated when you haven't. Keeping to a few rules can help. Get several estimates, and crosscheck them: you will spot what things have been left off one when you see them on another. Every single instruction should be written down and a carbon copy kept. Measure things yourself – all appliances, for example, are shown in the brochure flat against the wall, and stick out several more inches because their ugly innards protrude at the back. With shelves, do what I wished we'd done: draw them yourself on the wall.

I'll tell you another solution: just leave it as it is. All that dry rot you have to take out when you move in – the previous owner got on all right with it, didn't she? And if she could live with her wallpaper so, with the aid of a good pair of sunglasses, can you. Just keep your mind fixed on the frightful alternative and you'll find you can put up with anything.

They then moved, with decreasing enthusiasm, to the size of family she actually had. They explained about the population explosion, but the old lady just snorted, knowing that no one actually makes such a personal decision with reference to anything of that sort. They asked about her food bills and tutted at the vast quantities of bread and marge, the few and elusive proteins, that she actually got into her young. They were upset to find the children apparently slept three to a bed. They wondered, audibly, what the hell she thought she was at; and the children sat in a row on the toe and sang 'Shoe, sweet shoe'.

The old lady replied with some heat that the children preferred one another's jolly company to a lot of rot about scholarships, careful work with educational toys and First Steps in reading; that if she never had time to teach them anything it didn't matter because they taught each other. She said she liked it this way, that at least if you had enough children you weren't fussed with idiotic child care theories, and she pointed conclusively to the reason for it all: the old man, e'en now climbing unsteadily up the laces singing an unsuitable song.

*   *   *

We now have a situation where family planning gives everyone a choice; but good reasons for making the choice, or rejecting it, are still a matter of total guesswork. I could hardly track down a list of arguments, let alone experiments, that produced any firm conclusions about what you could expect from this or that sort of family. But it set me wondering what were the reasons that really do make people decide on their size of family.

Obviously the first thing is the sort of unit you want to live in. Parents of six must love not just children but living in a crowd; the mother copes not with one or two pernickety in-before the children came and after they'd grown – if, that is, they were still together by then. Americans, indeed, often seem to be so overwhelmed by their children that they'll do anything for them except stay married to the co-producer.

In this, the slum mother of seven who doesn't try waving a menstrual calendar at a drunken Irishman on a Saturday night, and the mobile wife who sticks at two children so that she can stick to her husband are doing exactly the same thing: paying as much attention to the marriage as to the results of it.

I think parents of any size family are actually doing what *they* want, and that none is being nobler than any other. And when you start being mean about other people's motives, there's always a first-class chance you've got it wrong. Witness the priest who called on a newly arrived mother of eleven, and went on for some time about the duties of holy motherhood, the blessings of a Christian family and how the Lord would provide. When he paused for breath the mother said, 'But Father, I'm not a Catholic.' 'Holy Mother of God!' he said. 'Then what are you – a sex-mad raving maniac or something?'

4 · *Growing Rotten Gracefully*

An Indian, asked to admire New Delhi during the British Raj, nodded appreciatively and said: 'Yes, this will make the noblest ruin of them all.' On the days when the fall of the year, the fall of bank balance and blood pressure remind us we will not last for ever, there is macabre pleasure in working out what sort of ruin one would like to be: how to collapse in comfort and decay in the grand manner.

Decay need not be unattractive. An ivy-twined statue with a broken nose, lichen scrawling across the marble cheek, is an improvement on its original form of 'Councillor Worthing 1858'. A garden run wild, the pergolas collapsed, roses returning to briar and a lone lily choked with weeds has something more than a row of neat ranunculas; no doubt the Sleeping Beauty was tempted to turn to the waking gardeners and say: 'No, leave it the way it is.'

But heaven save us from the deserted air-strip, from rusting barbed-wire round the abandoned Nissen hut; the peeling posters on the damp-stained wall, and machines that whirr once, sickeningly, when you kick them. In leather and wood, wine and teeth and bone and bronze something of soul survives; in the polythene bag and the disused factory only the form is indestructible.

So how to be leather and gold, and not a polythene old bag exciting only a pallid sympathy? The people who go to pieces with panache are often, one must admit, pretty awful: Aunt Ada Doom, still shrieking 'I saw something nasty in the woodshed!'; the aged Sarah Bernhardt, terrifying two generations of cringing attendants – these are the sort that are never going to shrink simply into a resentful boredom. To be lit from within by wild illusion is a help, maybe; which is why Ireland does such a good line in grand old scamps, every one a Behan character – as with the snug full of gross and watery-eyed old men of whom journalist Seamus Kelly said, as a blonde hipped her way past them, 'Outside every thin girl there's a fat man clamouring to be let in.'

The effect to be aimed at is of a flare overwhelmed by the elements: the impression that somehow drink and age and madness and gout have not extinguished the vital spark.

Progress, it has to be admitted, decays badly. The one survivor of a wild religion has dignity as the last man on earth in contact with God; but a mass movement of three old dears and a cracked piano, still fumbling the pamphlets of the New Dawn, has none.

Progressive people, too, had better stay undecayed: either they live as soft as anyone, tax dodging for elaborately moral reasons, or they stand where they always did - barefoot at the barricades, bewildered to see that the battle has moved to another street. Perhaps the saddest of all are the ones whose reform has actually happened, and hasn't worked; they have to watch miserably as time tracks back and abandons teacherless education, resumes the means test, gives up open-plan living. Advanced ideas get overtaken, but the opinions of a Peregrine Worsthorne will become you as well – nay, better – when you're ninety.

There are great possibilities, too, in being raddled – if you are only being raddled enough. It takes not just a limp rayon dress and a too bright lipstick, but spangles and a train and an awful old hat, flour face-powder and bootbrush eyelashes – then we have something of La Goulue in the gutter.

Where to stage your collapse? If you have no crumbling castle out of Thomas Peacock, the choice is a tricky one – for it is no good going to the bad in the wrong place. 'In New

York you may be café society, in Illinois you're just the town drunk' – but you can't even be the town drunk to any effect in Harlow, for instance, or a terrible old person in a place like Cheltenham, where there aren't enough juniors to go round. Paris probably answers well, they are so used to wild men haranguing them in cafés and sleeping curled up on the warm-air vents from the Metro; for myself I'd pick Aldgate East, where the Old Red Lion shelters the gayest of *les misérables*; they do a particularly good line in songsters of a bygone year who hold the microphone passionately to their lips – except that, having no teeth to speak of, it goes half-way down their throats and the voice comes out as a roar.

There was a young and beautiful girl, who was the great and good friend of some of the early psychoanalysts and latterly lived in Freud's house; in her old age she became totally bald and found it almost intolerable to have to do life without the power, any more, to charm. And she said to another young and beautiful girl, 'Remember me when the light goes out' – and the girl, now eighty, remembers only too well.

With the last flicker I would rather be a scandalous old scallywag who had to be dealt with than a reasonable being to be pitied and ignored; throwing a bottle through a church window the day before my funeral in a final bid for attention.

'Hell or heaven, here I come!'

5 · Survival of the Fattest

If you are all quite sure that the flood has subsided, the fire burned itself out and that the madman has left for the day, I will come out from under my desk and address you as usual. But not without a shiver: for I've just been reading a crisp, cheery little book, *The Book of Survival*, by Anthony Greenbank whose implications are even more alarming than its advice.

It sets out to tell you how to stay alive, not by the exercise of James Bond bravado, but by the correct deployment of your fat soft overcivilized self; how to survive in a dressing gown, with crying children, pregnant, or without your glasses. It ought to be reassuring to read about so many things you can do in a crisis; but the whole wide world of hazard wakes up and snarls at you as you leaf through it.

Some of it is first-aid and practical manual stuff; you punch a broken windscreen that has gone milky; you don't move broken limbs; it's insane to turn a warm doorhandle in a fire; if you've got frostbite you keep making faces to fight it (too bad for the mortician if it sets hard even so). Some of it, whatever the author thinks, is beyond the likes of most of us: I doubt if I could tie the knots to lower the injured from a height (any more than the Girl Guides so thought during our brief encounter), nor would I get far deflating my clothing to avoid being trapped against the roof of the pothole.

Though there is a lot more sense in it than in things like the one-in-five plan of the Civil Defence, who hope that one person in five will be able to set a candle in a flower-pot and make a cup of tea. People do have half-forgotten memories which might keep them alive in a crisis – things like not drinking sea-water, or remembering that the reason people in films sink into quicksands so fast is just because they throw up their arms – what they ought to do is to hurl themselves flat.

Servicemen are solemnly taught not to eat the liver of a polar bear lest they die of an excess of Vitamin A, and to leave its women alone; no doubt the bear in real life looks no more like the bear in the manual than the roast beef looks like the carving diagram, but at least the feeling that you can do *something* may help you to keep sane in an unimaginable situation. It should, at any rate, get you further than simply repeating the Victorian maxim: 'I am an Englishwoman; I was born in wedlock; I am standing on dry land.'

Yet the fear remains; and I realized as I thumbed through the book that I was enjoying it. 'We only ask to be reassured About the noise in the cellar And the window that should not have been open', they wince in *The Family Reunion*. We get the creeps, we get the misery, we get the pain even nowadays; what we don't get in the ordinary way is any stimulation from our miseries. We are the safe century; we put people quietly in gas ovens and shoot them by numbers in Siberia (six million apiece); people die and go mad and lead lives of quiet desperation, but the desperation is man-made and it provokes no man-made moral fibre to meet it. You may die in a motor smash, but there was no striding out to meet danger, no swashbuckling on of seat belts. The police, the insurance companies, the council will take care of everything; the old go back to hospital to die, the disabled stay home in the daytime; even the sheeted dead think twice before they shriek and gibber in the Roman streets.

Underneath our neat and tedious glooms there still does lie, like a river under a city, the respect and terrible fear of organic life: of the plague that flieth in darkness, of the wolf between the trees, of the eternal snows and the anvil of the sun.

I'm all for sneering, in a general way, at people who prattle of fall-out shelters and atom-proof attics; anything which encourages people to think another war can be survived might lead them to the lunatic notion that it might be won. But our spaces are small. I wonder if the Americans, with their vaster territory, are as crazed as we say when they speculate on, say, the survival chances of a fat pater-familias with a great stock of food as against God's own boy scout with a penknife and a flint.

Still, someone might survive. And it might well be someone who knew how to kill a deer without a gun, or find water deep underground, or make fire when everything was already burned. As A. P. Herbert says:

> *Then will survive a horse or two, I hope,*
> *A boy, with knife, some logs, a little rope.*
> *Then some young Chichester may hoist his main*
> *And sail away to start the world again.*

6 · Of Lice and Men

We hear all the time, from *McCall's* to the *New Statesman*, from the headmistresses' conference to the haunts of queers and places where they swing, what is wrong with modern woman. Everything from the weather to the state of the nation's teeth is blamed on women's changing status, lack of sexual identity, lack of motherly qualities or fitness for high executive position.

But modern man comes in for none of this bashing. If there is any suggestion that he may contain, here and there, a fault, the whole thing is immediately referred back to his home background and it's 'Don't blame me, blame mother' all over again. No one suggests that his utter lack of firmness in accepting responsibility for his own actions could ever perhaps be his own fault.

Men have always, of course, attempted to dump their moral responsibility in someone else's lap, from 'The woman tempted me and I did eat' onwards. 'You don't', as the social worker said, 'hear much about the problems of the unmarried father.' You might hear more if men thought past the girl to the problem of the baby; but they aren't taught about that because it isn't boys who get pregnant. Michael Schofield, in his survey of the sexual behaviour of teenagers, said 67 per cent of boys had never had any sex education at all, which shows just how little they have been taught about women.

Traditionally, of course, the moral teaching of boys – especially as plugged in O.K. boarding schools – has always been about their dealings with other men. You didn't desert a pal in the front line, sneak on another boy or steal his penknife; even when they got old enough to consider their dealings with women, it was only in their capacity as other people's property – someone else's wife or other feller's sisters (must have been quite a strain on the virtue of brotherless girls). 'Women are the game of England and morality is the gaming laws' just about expressed it; being a rake was entirely compatible with honour, though the cavalry phrase 'he loves and rides away' is a little less fine in its mechanized version: 'he simply screws and bolts'.

But at least the whole social framework did ensure that once you had taken the plunge and got married you were stuck with it: as you made your bed so did you lie on it – or worst had a bed made up in the dressing-room. Nobody said, 'There, there, dear, it was just a boyish mistake' and got you out of it: nobody thought that if you shut your eyes and took a deep breath your wife and children would simply disappear like spots before the eyes.

Yet that is often what I feel the softies of the modern age expect. You get otherwise intelligent and kindly men (no, of course, not *all*) believing a load of optimistic nonsense that simply takes your breath away. They talk as if, by simply turning up on Sundays and paying a few bills, you can be a 'good father' although you've smashed your children's background into splinters.

They fall for a girl in nightclub situations, get bored with the sight of their wives at the sink, and think they are making a fair comparison, that the girl will curl her false eyelashes even over early-morning tea. They are liberal enough to sympathize, when talking about a distressed friend or a criminal, with the problems of children of broken homes – and then go right ahead and organize a broken home for their own.

I've noticed, too, that any film/TV documentary/play about the problems of cracking marriages (directed by men) always assumes that the problem is the same for both sexes, so that they may as well show a man sobbing his heart out as a woman. This splendid bit of wishful thinking rules out entirely what happens *after* the divorce, where, like Dorothy Parker's soldier's wife, the woman can say, 'You've got all of a new life, I've got half an old one.'

It ignores the fact that you cannot get two families out of the same income without somebody suffering – guess who? That after twenty years' hard a woman is not as remarriageable as a man of the same age; and that our social set-up may confine such a woman to all-female company for years – unless, of course, she has a pretty face or a job. They tick us off for having jobs instead of that utter dependence on our males which makes for harmony in the home – but can you blame us, when they aren't dependable?

The biggest sentimentality of all is the idea that if anyone is attracted elsewhere, it must be his wife's fault anyway. Even the Marriage Guidance Council fosters this by suggesting that other women are a symptom and not a disease; women's mags keep plugging it to reassure their readers; and even those women whose husbands are still among those present, are inclined to blame the wife instead of saying 'There but for the grace of God' (or my personal version of that, which is to say 'If *my* husband can stick *me* I don't know what you lot are grumbling about').

Without the conviction that you are *committed* to your wife and family, an *affaire* may lead to a break-up, unless there is a strong moral resolution against it. And strong moral resolution is exactly what these busters are weak on: they behave as if they couldn't help themselves, as if they had no say in what happens to them, as if all they could have been expected to promise was 'for richer, for better, in health'. A promise isn't a promise if you can keep it only when you feel like it; without a promise – and a man capable of keeping one – the most married woman in the land is no better off than those nuts in the Colour Magazine recently who had rejected marriage because they had missed the point of it altogether.

Jonathan Miller has made an immensely shrewd point about the new determinism: that the knowledge, albeit vulgarized and misunderstood, that peoples' decisions are influenced by factors far back in their upbringing has weakened the amount of resolution anyone is ready to deploy: if you're not fully responsible for your failings you don't rate full credit for your virtues either, so why try?

Yet people do try. People do behave marvellously in grim situations. I can think of a man who has cooked every meal for his disabled wife for years; I knew one who remained married, in the fullest sense of the word, to someone who was not only the wrong someone but the wrong sex; I can think of several men who have coped magnificently and for years with wives who have 'odd' patches of depression and difficulty. Perhaps they don't make the ones who walk out seem more wicked than before; but heavens, they make them seem feeble.

In all my fifty-seven variations (some of them printable) on the slogan 'the family that prays together stays together' my favourite is the least amusing: the family that stays together stays together. And I would like, just once, to hear someone say of a man who had left, left, left his wife and four fat babies in the middle of the kitchen floor, *not* that he's been through a hard time lately, or that his mother was a very complicated woman, or that he's worried about his job, or that he married very young; but simply 'You louse'.

7 · *Conversations I can do Without*

'Well, anyway, I said that if he was going to take that line I just wasn't going to go out with him again; and then he went off and danced for *half an hour* with that dreadful girl with the red hair – you know, the one whose bra straps show but whose bosom doesn't; and when he came back he came right up to me and took my arm . . . honest, I could have *died*. . . .'

*   *   *

'Marvellous chap. He turned me into a tax loss in the Bahamas and both the wife and I got new Jags last year. If you're making enough, I'll put you in touch with him – no, happy to, no trouble at all.'

*   *   *

'. . . and the first day you just eat cucumbers and you're allowed two cups of black coffee and the second day you have four ounces of steak for breakfast and . . .'

*   *   *

'Oh, *may* I look at your baby? Isn't he sweet – tuck-tuck-tuck-tuck – there, he's smiling at me. Yes, he is. Yes, you are my poppet. Oh, the dear – did horrid Mummy go out to work and leave you then; here, give me another smile. Give me BIG smile. You know, it's funny, they *all* smile at me!'

*   *   *

'Here, Rufus – come here – RUFUS – come HERE – oh, God, now he's out of the gate: Come here boy – good boy – come here – RUFUS, WILL YOU COME HERE AT ONCE, SIR. . . .'

'. . . anyway Greg – that's Gregory Peck – just couldn't *stand* this director, so Audrey – you know, Audrey Hepburn – got in touch with Hitch, who was doing this thing with Bob – Bob Mitchum, of course – and the Duke – you know they call John Wayne "Duke" – and he said . . .'

*   *   *

'But you can't buy one of *those* – the back axle falls off.'

'It's not as bad as *that*. Anyway, it's got the trailing-wishbone anti-synchromesh suspension, and you'd have to pay five hundred more to find that in any other car.'

'I grant you that, and I like the three-barrelled updraught carbs, but I know a chap who drove one in a rally and he wouldn't touch one again.'

'Well, *I* know the chap who designed the thing – not well, mind you – and he reckoned they were five years ahead of anybody else with their dialectical toothless gearbox.'

*   *   *

'It's only a minor exhibition, but I do feel he's moving away from his abstract empathy to the appreciation of new spatial values and a deeper relationship of tone.'

*   *   *

'Is that you, Mary? Look, I seem to be in the Rose and Crown – it turns out to be Freddie's birthday. You know Freddie – you must know him. Terribly nice chap. I'll tell you all about him. It's rather sad, really, so I feel I *ought* to be sort of propping him up. I suppose you can't get down here because of the kids? Well, anyway, I mean I may be a bit late for dinner. Look – you just go ahead and eat it, and I'll pick up a sandwich or something. And I'll tell you all about Freddie when I get in. Don't stay up if you want to get some sleep.'

'Look, I'm not suggesting *anything* – I'd just like us to *sleep* together, that's all – just sleep, nothing else. I just think it would be rather marvellous to wake up in the morning and find you beside me . . . God, you're inhibited, anyone would think I was trying to rape you or something. . . .'

* * *

'. . . and I was in the second stage before the doctor even got there, with the contractions coming every minute and a half, and the midwife said . . .'

* * *

'Yes, lovely thanks – gorgeous little place, completely un-spoiled, nothing there at all except the three hotels and this little bar down by the beach – wine's a shilling a bottle and cigarettes twenty-five for sixpence; no, we only had upset tummies for about three days. . . .'

* * *

'. . . it's not that *I* mind, I believe in letting them lead their own lives entirely, if she wants to come in at three in the morning that's all right by me so long as she's up at seven as usual the next day; but then I started finding these most extraordinary letters actually *in her bed* and she flew into the most terrible Sicilian tantrum. . . .'

* * *

'Why are you putting flowers in that jug?'
  'To make the house look pretty for Danny.'
  'Why?'
  'Because I like her.'
  'Why?'
  'She's so nice to us – nice to you too.'
  'Why?'

32

'Because she likes you.'

'Why?'

'I HAVEN'T THE FAINTEST IDEA. SHE MUST BE OFF HER BLOODY HEAD.'

8 · Changing my Mind

A Bernard Hollowood cartoon once showed a TV discussion with one man saying, brokenly: 'Yes, yes; you're quite right; I've been wrong all these years.' Unlikely though it seems that anyone who sounds off for a living should ever admit it, Pope was probably right when he said that the man who said he had changed his mind was simply saying: 'I am wiser today than I was yesterday.'

Some changes are easier to admit than others, however. I have changed my mind readily enough about green stamps and plastic daffodils. I've changed my mind radically about nature conservancy; I still think people come first, but nowadays it seems that the best understanding we have of ourselves may come from studies of animals in their own homes and not just scratching moodily in zoos. And I even have to admit, though it goes greatly against the grain, that I have changed my mind about sport.

I used to think the only use for it was to give small boys something else to kick besides me, and that the sooner our over-civilized bodies became too atrophied to need any, the better I would be pleased. But that was before I had any idea of the ritualizing of aggressive drives; before I realized that wanting to be better than the next team along was something more than an expression of adolescent insecurity; that thug-like youths are better employed throwing a javelin than a hand grenade; *and that they have to throw one or the other.* Before I read Lorenz's *On Aggression.* Before I read Robert Ardrey's *The Territorial Imperative.*

It's impossible to put Ardrey's book into an article, so I can

34

only state its conclusions and let people look for the proof to the book itself. But baldly, Ardrey makes two fundamental points, and demonstrates them by study after fascinating study of various kinds of animals. The first point is that as well as the instincts we all know about – fear and hunger and the various instincts of reproduction – there is another: an instinct for territory. It is to defend their territory that most animals band together, in pairs or in hundreds; it is outside pressure from the next tribe along that makes them behave in amity towards one another. It is this instinct developed, Ardrey argues, that forms the real basis of our moral sense: our impulse to sink our interests to the common good, to do desperate things, even to die, for people other than ourselves.

His second major point is that the three things creatures need are security, stimulation and identity – and that security on the whole comes *last*. For identity, some animals have a pecking order, some men have army rank; 007 has his number, the executive his status carpet; sex is a means to identity rather than vice versa. Stimulation comes second; if necessary stimulation by fighting. Just as a Siamese fighting fish glows with his true colours only when measuring up to an enemy of his own species, so men without rivalry may also droop, lose purpose and decay. He proves, to my mind conclusively, that the need for stimulation is so vital that people will throw over safety and prosperity, kindness and everything of apparent worth rather than suffer the ultimate fate worse than death, which is boredom.

You need to have been a thorough-going progressive, of course, for this to hit you in the solar plexus as it hit me. People of my intellectual generation grew up exposed to just about all the *tabula rasa* theories going. There was the economic one: people would all work together in peace and cheerfulness for the common good if only the system hadn't set them against one another; once remove private property, and greed and competitiveness would go too. There was the psychological one: children had their aggressions forced upon them by frustration, their traumas pounded into them by insensitive and uncaring parents.

With all the fervour with which the ancients looked to the golden age or Rousseau to the noble savage, we believed in the noble babe: and reckoned that nothing but environment mucked him up. When the environment seemed to improve out of all recognition and people stayed much as before we either (in the manner of those sacrificing ever more frantically to their ancestors as the charms fail to work) demanded a more and more perfect environment, or became as disillusioned as every revolutionary always has been at finding that the last thing people want is liberty, equality, fraternity.

Of course, plenty of people were cynical about these ideals from the start: it is not sinners this man comes to call, but the righteous to repentance. But just as people who had grown up believing that sexual instincts were wicked and carnal and only a painful necessity for producing children were released beyond measure by the Freudian revelation of their absolutely basic importance, so we are now released – those of us who have felt guilty every time we enjoyed our own property, bewildered at all the men who adore the trappings of war, miserable because every rehoused set of underdogs instantly tries to become top dogs of the kennel, or simply uncomprehending of the amount of sheer pleasure one seems to get from battling with one's enemies.

The desire to have and to hold, to screech at the neighbours and say 'Mine, all mine' is in our nature too. Ardrey and his allies have let us off perfection and I for one feel a lot better for it.

Already there have been cries of dismay from people who say that to admit all this is to give a great old boost to the fascists and reactionaries. Socially, I don't see it: if you finally see why you mind so much about your own garden and latchkey, it ought to make you angrier than ever on behalf of people with no home at all. And politically, Ardrey says it is exactly the opposite. To date, the dictators have the edge on the rest of us because they have been the only ones answering these needs – offering a uniform, an outlet, a stirring of the blood and a feeling of *us* and *they*. 'Why do you people act like there's a war on?' says Doc in *West Side Story* – because there's no respectable outlet for the instincts that war satisfies. As Tinbergen says, the less we understand about our own instincts, the more we are their victim.

Everyone from Aesop on has read back into the animal world his own pet theories of life: now at last we are taking a proper look at animals – and, through them, ourselves. Philosophically speaking, it seems likely that what zoology and the physical sciences were to the end of the nineteenth century, Freud's discoveries were to the first half of the twentieth, animal ethology will be to the second half.

It may be that the present explorers will turn out to be only the beginners. But in the meantime, a light has been switched on in another part of the room; and nothing will ever look the same again.

9 · *Are You Sitting Comfortably?*

The odd thing about committees is that although you never meet, outside the fortunate ranks of the zoo and the nursery school, anyone who doesn't sit on them, you never meet anyone who approves of them either. From the Cabinet to the West Whittling Oyster-catchers Water Pollution Sub-committee, we run our affairs by getting together in huddles; and wherever two or three are gathered together at all, the same sort of charades go on.

Some committees are a write-off from the start. Any committee that meets no oftener than twice a year is hopeless: the deadline is so far off that everyone promptly forgets what they promised to do until the night before the next meeting, when there is no time for anything except the construction of a really good excuse.

Large committees are also useless: like large worm pills, they contain far too much filler. Filler are the people who are there to represent something – women or mathematics or the management – rather than because they're interested; or they are the sort of driftwood that actually likes sitting about in a hat and chatting. The most devastating give-away I ever heard was when it was suggested that a large social work committee was not the best place to sort out individual cases. 'But without the casework,' said the bewildered chairman, 'what would my committee *do*?'

Any committee that is the slightest use is composed of people who are too busy to want to sit on it for a second longer than they have to. It follows that the more that can be done outside the committee room the better. A chairman who nobly lets himself be moaned to at home by the emotional can save half an hour of the committee's time at the cost of his own. Written stuff that is sent round beforehand not only allows people to read it at home – it prevents their reading it there and then in committee. '*Never* let a committee do any drafting,' one chairman told me. 'Get one man to write it, and have it most beautifully typed – if it all looks neat and virginal no one will feel like ravishing it. Not in front of the committee anyway.'

As Parkinson says, in any large committee everything is fixed up by the two ablest men over a lunch – and when this happens the relevant question is whether the committee need meet at all.

All newspaper offices, and I suspect others, go on a sort of committee cycle. For three weeks running it turns out that two people have commissioned the same article, and a committee is set up to keep everybody in touch with and responsible for everything else. For a few weeks you bring your ideas to the committee; then you reckon to have them at the committee; after that you just sit there and wait to get back to work. More intimate committees are formed to bypass or reinforce the first; suddenly it is clear that there are only three and a half hours in the working week when there isn't a committee going on; someone writes 'Communication is the Thief of Time' angrily in the lift with a lipstick; and we go back to square one, no committees.

Chairmanship is crucial. All good chairmen are masters at laying the fuses of an agenda. There are only two places where people actually decide anything useful: during the first half-hour and the last. So a shrewd chairman gets rid of half a dozen minor but necessary items to start with, then gives everyone a chance to show off: 'Something like whether magazines should be borrowed from the library,' said one vice-chancellor. 'They *like* that.' You can whistle without difficulty through anything at the end, when everyone is wondering if they're going to make the early train; the wasted time is usually in the middle of the afternoon, when people drone round and round the subject like sleepy wasps, never quite making for the open window.

The person who liberates a committee from this particular fix is often the secretary. One Government secretary I worked with admits quite openly that when he found we'd argued for hours and decided nothing, he put into the minutes the conclusion he thought we had arrived at and simply waited to see if anyone queried it.

His other canny techniques included a flurry of inactivity in which he extinguished the more far-fetched of our proposals whenever it was absurd to do either nothing or something; and the casual way he would manage to ring us up, usually about something quite different, to remind us what it actually *was* we had so eagerly agreed to do. Indeed, the difference between a good committee and a bad one, in most cases, is the difference between 'Let it be done!' and 'Joe will do it by Tuesday.'

A good chairman, too, has to be pretty Machiavellian – though most are too shrewd to *appear* to be so. One chairman of some boys' charity does it all with gin – anyone can say anything for an hour; then he stands them huge drinks and they waft out without the slightest idea of what it is they have agreed to.

'How do you stop people muttering among themselves?' I asked one. 'Put them opposite you,' he said promptly. 'Then they've got to say it to you. The loud ones at the end – there's no trouble about hearing them.' 'How do you get the garrulous to shut up?' I asked another. 'You don't,' he said. 'At least not at once. Otherwise they spend all the time thinking of what they'd have liked to say instead of listening.'

When all's said and done, though, a good chairman can

only lead. A committee may have, as they say, no heart to appeal to and no arse to kick; but if it gels as it should, it does assume a sort of corporate personality. And this is what it is really all about: a way of using more talents at once than any one man has. A camel is a horse designed by a committee, yes – but it's always possible that a workable, indestructible, water-carrying animal with sandproof feet was actually what was wanted; and that the camel will outlast the solitary chevalier.

10 · Rules of the Game

Five rules for maddening your man:

1. Count ten and take a deep breath before you say anything harsh. This will enable you to perfect the wording.

2. Begin sentences: 'Oh, I meant to tell you yesterday that . . .' (the office rang, mother's coming, the car was almost out of petrol).

3. End sentences (if about the rates, the space race, compost for the clematis or other unallied subjects), 'After all, we've got to think of the children.'

4. Keep one grievance in reserve; do not be caught by 'No buttons on these pyjamas!' without 'What about the screws on the bedroom mirror?'

5. Draw in the breath sharply through closed teeth every time he overtakes on a clear main road an antique Austin doing 20 m.p.h.

Five rules for getting your own back:

1. Appear in your oldest suit ten minutes before you are both due out for dinner; say bravely, 'No, it's *my* fault: I should have reminded you to press my good one.' (Watch the timing.)

2. Remember her birthday late enough to make sure she feels forlorn, but just too early for her to enjoy a splendid scene over it.

3. When you aren't listening to what she is saying, say 'What seems to be the trouble, then?' every ten sentences; if silence indicates that a response really is expected, say incredulously '*What* did you just say?'

4. Put used matches back in the kitchen box so that she finds nothing but duds when she comes to light the Christmas pudding.

5. Wait till she has got the early tea tray, shut up the cats, locked up, taken her face off, filled the kettle and settled into bed with a sigh. Then say, 'I wonder – do you think I could have a bit of cheese and pickle?'

Five rules for demolishing Professor X:

1. Say that his brand-new theory 'revives the old idea that . . .'

2. Quote an authority who says, 'There is no evidence for his theory'. Take care to select an authority writing before the evidence was collected.

3. Get hold of his early works, bribing his tutor if necessary; then refute him out of his own mouth.

4. Get him off his own good ground: if he's right about the habits of apes, switch to the question of the cages he keeps them in; if he knows the source of the Amazon, denounce him from the point of view of missionary work in Argentina.

5. If he is dead right in every way, jeer at his earnestness.

Five rules for mothers:

1. To avoid being shamed by the precocious children of others, always give your own children's ages as six months less than they are.

2. Have the life-saving drink before the children's bedtime, not after.

3. Remember that in our society mothers take the place elsewhere occupied by the Fates, the System, Negroes, Communism or Reactionary Imperialist Plots; mothers go on getting blamed until they're eighty, but shouldn't take it personally.

4. Remember that children and zip fasteners do not respond to force.

5. Except occasionally.

Five rules for the elderly:

1. Don't say, 'I'm just a silly old woman.' Some of the young are fool enough to believe you.

2. Don't hunt round your mouth with your tongue for forgotten pieces of food.

3. Take the advice that surgeon Dickson Wright gave to the Distressed Gentlefolk: take a drink and have a flutter when the occasion offers itself.

4. Read Dean Swift's *Resolutions for When I Come to be Old* – for example the one 'Not to be over severe with young People, but give Allowances for their youthfull follyes, and Weeknesses'.

5. On the pattern of the Red Queen believing three impossible things before breakfast, try to approve of one modern innovation a week.

Five rules for the conduct of Christmas:

1. Try to make the presents cost as much as the wrapping paper.

2. On Christmas Day, send everyone, large or small, crying or cheerful, drunk or sober, separately or together, to bed for the afternoon.

3. If your path to the shops is blocked by a group of youths in beards, moustaches, Afghanistan jackets and grubby cotton caftans (as worn at Arnold Wesker's Round House) ask sweetly if they are doing a Nativity play.

4. Remember that if you forget to spend several pounds on nuts, sweets, dates, mince and muscatels, no one will, in fact, notice.

5. Realize that if you want to do the shopping all in one

day, or by post, or all through charities, or not at all, you can; so stop groaning about what a sweat Christmas is when you know you're loving every moment of it.

One rule for children:
  Shout before seven
  Get socked by eleven.

11 · *The Unattraction of Opposites*

'What's the opposite of black?' says a six-year-old. 'White.'
'What's the opposite of running?' 'Standing still.' 'What's
the opposite of standing on one leg?' 'Standing on both?' '*No*,
silly – standing on the other!' Loud laughs for all the family.
Still, the child has a point: that you can often have a choice of
opposites, and that while there are obviously only two alternatives, there may be a third choice shyly in eclipse behind one of them.

Take, for example, the way people rate women. Men used
to have endless boring discussions about whether these should
be Beautiful or Useful; 'Looks don't last, cooking do,' said
the cracker-barrel sages, and the rival merits of peach pie and
cheesecake kept them going for hours. Or they stamped them
as Young or Old, and got as far as Benjamin Franklin's appalling reasons for choosing 'to make an old woman happy,
rather than a young one miserable' ('Besides, they are so
grateful').

Nowadays we're all supposed to be young and beautiful,
nobody gets away with being a lousy cook except film stars,
and they simply argue about whether we should be useful in
a job or around the house. I would say 'with or without
education' except that the argument is at its strongest over
American college girls; and they, it is known, are exposed to
education in much the same way as gin is exposed to vermouth in the perfect Martini: you lock the bottle in a cupboard
and carry the vermouth past it once a week.

Colleges themselves are full of opposites. At Cambridge
you used to have undergraduates or Magdalene men, the

latter living on the same side of the Cam as their horses and hounds; it is said that many of them never crossed the river all the time they were up. Oxford or Cambridge, it once was; then it was Oxbridge or Redbrick; Jimmy Porter added White Tile and now, with the Lasdun and Spence campuses, it's that or Streaked Concrete. From being Classics or Modern Side (a term still used by the old school to disparage those who'd never make the grade with Plato) it is now a matter of Arts v. Scientists, Footballers v. Jazz or simply Sociology v. the rest.

International oppositions shift constantly. Remember when Russia was the opposite of America, and they hadn't invented the Chinese Bomb? And take Scotland. I was at school there during the war and well remember copying down one short paragraph of the benefits accruing to Scotland from the Union of the Parliaments, followed by pages and pages and pages of the benefits to England; there was no question of the England v. Scotland struggle being dwarfed in any way by the current squabble with Germany and Japan. We think of ourselves as the absolute opposite of, say, Sicilians, and belonging to the luke-warm Nordic group; but to a Norwegian we may be the exact opposite of everything he knows – indeed, one such actually said what fun it was in London, among a warm-blooded southern people.

You see parents trying to arrange the opposition to reflect well on their own child: 'Tom's quite happy playing by himself all morning; now Sue, she's just the opposite – clings to her mother's skirts all the time.' Sue's mother, of course, would probably point out that her Sue is no trouble, sleeps through till eight every morning, while Tom gets his poor mother up half the night. At least we use the same categories as our contemporaries – take the thing back a generation or two and you're not even doing that. We talk about whether a child is or isn't difficult with his food; yet I heard the grandmother of my feeding problem congratulate him the other day on the virtue of Not Being Greedy.

Again, a century ago a good husband was one who provided for you, the opposite one who didn't. None of them helped in the house and if they helped in bed you didn't discuss it. Now the whole thing seems to hinge on whether he helps with the washing up, this being the only quality to interrupt a straightforward opposition of the sexy and the stooges.

Not, of course, that it is only with husbands that the rating varies with time and place: few misunderstandings are more opaque than those between, say, an Arab rating people on courage or cowardice and an American assessing whether they are or are not advanced in technology. And when my mother once said that her mother thought my other grandmother rather low-class for being a Wee Free and not a United Presbyterian, my father said, 'Very possibly; but *my* mother thought *your* mother loose on points of theology.'

What is so encouraging about looking at other people's opposition is the effect it has on one's own: when apparently jammed in a two-prong dilemma there may always be a third way of assessing things. Either men must live in the stinking cities or stick to the purity of the village pump – only then they invented main drainage. If it isn't Catholicism, it must be Communism – only it mustn't, because they are both much more like each other than either is like liberalism, anarchy or sense. We have to sacrifice either the motor-car or our way of life – but they may yet invent a collapsible motor-car or personal locomotion on the lines of atom-powered roller-skates. When faced with two horrible alternatives (Republican and Democrat, Labour or Tory, Los Angeles or Bust) it's always worth trying for a third, which may make the first two seem like Tweedledum and Tweedledee.

Is the opposite of Hugh Trevor-Roper Tacitus or A. J. P.

Taylor? Is the opposite of claret burgundy? Or the opposite of both Ribena? Or the opposite of those, biscuits? Or the opposite of booze and biscuits coke? Or the opposite of all such material things Yoga and the theory of relativity? It all depends how you set it up. The opposite of 'must', as foreigners have to find out, is not 'must not' but 'need not'; and it's always a great comfort to reflect that the opposite of 'unbending' is 'unbending'.

12 · *Wide Awake Ideas on Dream Holidays*

Not everybody suffering from brochuritis, that epidemic which carries off thousands every year, is going to face quite the let-down of Mrs Anne Markle, who was promised a thousand-mile sea-cruise for a honeymoon and spent it in the bottom of a chest of drawers. But in your heady flirtation with the brochures, you ought to have it clear in your mind what your expectations are.

Some of the risks are predictable. People are going to seize eagerly on holidays offering them fourteen days on the Costa Brava for twenty quid including air fare – and then be amazed that their charter plane is held up behind the regular flights, and that their rooms, except in grossly overbuilt ex-fishing villages, do not look out on sea. They're more likely to end up saying, if they are as determined to be delighted as one child I know of, 'Oh, look – a lovely *green* gasworks!'

Millions, too, are going to believe that the sun is bound to shine on their chosen British beach. It never seems to strike them that if the sun lived up to their expectations *every* year we'd have to have a quite different climate and landscape – brown grass, fire risks and fig trees. Yet because once in ten years they do get a heat wave, they spend the other nine playing draughts in the bar parlour in their only pair of warm trousers. Only sailors do all right, since the magical phrase 'It's always fresh out to sea' enables them to wear enough sweaters without loss of face.

And people often won't own up to what they really want.

One grey-haired lady I know of does, and railways round Italy stopping off for odd nights with virile porters. Others who want the same thing are quite likely to end up in staid resorts crammed only with German children and well-watched husbands; then they wonder why their dreams never came true. Many want what is plainly impossible – an unspoiled village the travel agents have heard of, or a chunk of real local life – but by the sea; a thing you actually get only in ports like Toulon. And the ones who account for the Mediterranean tea-and-chips trade *think* they want the foreign flavour; but actually couldn't be more petrified of it if the chef came out of the kitchen with a ray-gun saying 'I am a garlic'.

They are also not honest about the company they keep – to their great credit, no doubt. Husbands and wives don't want to admit that three weeks doing nothing in each other's company is a drag (second honeymoons are almost always disastrous unless, of course, the first was such a flop that it gains from the contrast); close friends honestly believe that they can share the housekeeping in a villa and still stay on speaking terms.

One way round the first trouble is to do at least some of your jaunts separately; even if you don't quarrel in museums the way we do (the echoes are magnificent) it's a lot easier to have something to say at the end of the day than to slog round trying to think of comments like the photographer's instructions: 'Brighter – brighter – BRIGHTER! Ah, too bright. Moisten the lips and start again.' And one family I know has got round the other problem by holidaying in the same town as their friends but not in the same house. Someone to gossip to on beach and bar stool, but not to meet at breakfast. It seems to work.

You can come hideous croppers by not noticing that your children have broken an age barrier. Tots who dug happily in the sand for seven years suddenly yearn for the bright lights and a pop group, babies who were casually breast-fed in car parks and quarries now require you to heat horrible little tins over a damp twig fire (no wonder the nomads keep up breast-feeding for five years: it's the only bit of equipment that you can't leave behind at the last place).

And all too many holidays are the wrong length. A fortnight is just too long for a frenetic weekend sort of relaxation, too short to come unwound all over the floor like a broken clock and still have time to put yourself together again. To my mind, the best thing to do with two weeks is to turn it into three long weekends, with three exciting fresh starts; makes it seem longer, too.

But holidays crash, I'm convinced, because people really believe they want to do nothing; and don't realize that doing nothing successfully takes years of practice. Some leisure activities are pretty hard work, fortunately: tennis and sailing and the Tour de France; those with none such just moon about buying sun-cream and waiting for the next meal. Cartier Bresson went out with a camera once to see what happened at a resort at six in the morning; he found tea-stands going for all those who had woken automatically at their normal time and didn't know what to do.

All our silly talk about the rat race obscures the fact that most men are sustained by their work even if they hate it, like the banana-necked women whose necks break if you take off the rings. Men mostly like their wives and families as an adjunct, not an occupation; the only people who adore holidays with their children are people like Paul Jennings, who adore having them around all the time anyway.

Of course there are holidays that work – people who go back and back to the same place or district, or stay long enough to get to know the score and almost develop a second way of life for summer. Short holidays for the wretchedly tired are all right, preferably beginning with a sea voyage: slow boat to Sweden, or Spain reached via Gibraltar: so are journeys with a purpose, like seduction or the search for scarabs.

But for many, it's off to a new place, a new hope and a new disillusion. You see yourself being, or being with, the bikini creatures in the TV ads; you spend your time with the same old tummy as at home. You do not become, as subconsciously you wished to become, the Emperor Franz Josef in Vienna, D. H. Lawrence in the Gulf of Spezia, a simple fisherman on the islands of the blessed. You are just one more sightseer in a sports shirt, looking for a place to sit down.

Hazlitt said that a holiday was the only sort of cake that makes bread eat better after it; it could be because we all actually prefer bread anyway.

13 · Death is Here to Stay

From the man who said that if they were going to die he hoped they'd die quickly so that we'd have less pulsating pictures on the telly, to the one who said he'd rather have his daughter die than walking around with a borrowed heart, there seems to have been nobody who hasn't had their say about organ transplants; each one of them no doubt feeling, as I do, that all the others have failed to get to the heart of the matter.

Two fears particularly seem to me wide of the mark. There's the worry that mere medical keenness might snuff us out early if we were needed to fill someone else's long-felt want. Of course, hospitals make mistakes; and they also have a marked disposition to prescribe whatever the surgeons happen to be best at; but the crashing damages for such a speed-up would surely make them warier than ever on a thing like this – let alone the extra scrutiny it will obviously attract.

And there's the idea that a tyranny might well use the technique to reinforce their Gauleiters with the innards of the innocent. Certainly a century that disposed of six million Trotskyites on the one hand and six million Jews on the other can hardly claim to have outgrown its loathsomeness; but I don't see how having your heart used for a transplant is going to be any worse for the murdered than, say, having it torn throbbing from your body as in the ancient Aztec amusement.

What intrigues me is that almost all the discussion about keeping people alive by unlikely means has been about the risk of someone dying when they had a chance to live; and none about the risk of people living when they should be allowed to die. Of course, the theory is that no one should ever die if they can possibly be kept going; but considering the circumstances in which people can linger on, this seems to me strange. People don't actually die less than they used to (well, obviously); they only die later and lonelier, and usually having to pretend that death doesn't happen at all.

This is not due to our humanity. So long as people stay alive somehow we don't much care what happens to them. We haul them out of car crashes and spend months repairing their bones and burns; if they then live out their lives as scarred vegetables indifferently cared for in wheelchairs, that's not our worry. We dump the aged in geriatric wards, and lest they endanger the lives we're so set on preserving we take away all the things that make life tolerable – the teeth, glasses and hearing aids of their five senses. I often feel our attitude to the aged is exactly like that of those who used to brick up nuns in walls – but with water and bread, so that they wouldn't be guilty of killing them.

So keen on keeping everyone alive are we that we hush up the facts of death; the Americans with their deep freezes and embalmings, we with our resolute practical determination not to ritualize death or to mourn.

And we have an extraordinary squint about suicide. Even the most humane studies talk only about preventing it, never assessing it; only Eustace Chesser, of all people, suggests in 'Living with Suicide' that sometimes the suicide can be right. We are equally appalled at the young girl who throws away a life that's barely started, and the sensible woman of seventy who wrote recently in the *Observer* that she did not intend to outlive her faculties if she could help it.

Part of the horror is atavistic, no doubt; and for the religious there's a clear obligation to spend your life and not squander it – work in a plague area, yes; a running jump off the cliff, no. But surely our repugnance at anyone ending his life like this would make a lot better sense if we had any normal notion of how a life should end. What are we supposed to hope for? An oxygen tent? In bed at home? The humane bolt-from-the-blue heart attack? Or the reflective death, calm, knowing, all passion spent? We not only have no idea of a good suicide as had the Japanese and the Romans, we have no idea of a good death either. We take our sick to hospital to die, instead of fetching them home; we keep the children away. Death is to us as sex was to the Victorians, taboo.

So we have the remarkable situation that the generation which has, more than any before it, assumed control over the moment and kind of death, has actually less familiarity with it than any generation before – familiarity even with its symptoms, let alone its significance. We behave as if the problem had ceased to exist for those for whom religion no longer solves it. Yet all we have done is to ensure that it always comes as a blinding surprise, that we make no preparation for it, and that we have no measure by which to decide when life is simply not worth living.

At this point I can see a vast misunderstanding rearing its huge, bewildered head. 'But surely you're not suggesting euthanasia . . . handing the old folk the hemlock . . . encouraging doctors to cut off the crippled in their prime . . . ?' No indeed. There are no possible safeguards that could even begin to balance the hazard of letting people legally put others out of their misery. But this isn't a question of law. We're so used to ending every discussion: 'There oughta be a law' that we forget the situations that are not of law but attitude. And in all this, we have only one attitude: we leave it to the doctors.

56

I imagine the doctors detest this but that they do take decisions of life and death is undeniable. Only a handful speed the going of the very senile, but I've spoken to plenty who have had to decide when to pull out the plugs and pronounce a patient hopeless; and a friend of mine was asked about his defective baby: 'Do we feed this baby or not?' – to which he gave the only possible answer: 'If there's enough doubt in your mind to ask me, then the answer's yes.' The fuss about the notices about resuscitating the over sixty-fives was a fuss, surely, not about this kind of decision being taken; but about such agonizing human responsibility becoming a matter of obeying the regulations.

I am convinced that leaving it to the doctors is no sort of answer. The whole medical profession is, quite simply, a tool – a brilliant, dedicated and intensely hard-working tool for preserving life. For those who have the means of life to decide whether you and I should live makes no better sense than that gunmakers – who have the means of death – should decide whether you or I should die. We have got to start having our own view of life and death again. Somehow we've got to get death back into the conversation, stop sheltering children from any faintest contact with it; work out what things we would die for, the things without which we would not care to go on living.

There are certain pointers left: the mothers, casually commented on in a famine report, who die first because they give their food to the children; or those burning Buddhist monks who, however absurd their cause, must have given millions a lift at the idea that anyone cares that much about anything. People who know what's worth dying for must know what's worth living for too; having got the measure of death they have got the measure of life.

When I was small I used to plan my deathbed, when I would gather my enemies around me and madden them with my forgiveness; now I suppose I would be offering them my tonsils as a parting present. But whatever it is, we need an idea of death that defines the terms on which we live. Maybe the answer *is* on any terms at all – though I doubt it. And if anyone says I don't know anything about it, I'd agree – but how come that I can get half-way through my life *without* knowing? To those who have never lost anyone close, death is a disaster headline, a rabbit squashed on the road, a covered shape lifted into the ambulance. It isn't enough.

14 · *Publish and be Damned*

Twice a year, in spring and autumn, publishers put out their catalogues of forthcoming books. . . .

* * *

The New Oxbridge Translation of the Bible

Several years ago a team of priests and parsons from all denominations gathered together to create a new version of the Bible more in tune with modern everyday life. This volume, taken from the original Greek and Hebrew texts but coloured by their own experiences in the poorer parishes of Britain, must make an impact on every reader: as when Christ drives the merchants from the temple with the words: 'Piss orf, yer racketeering gits.' Although this may strike an assonant chord in those familiar with the King James version, they cannot deny that it makes religion as simple and understandable as the working man's baked beans and beer.

Vietnam; Triumph or Tragedy? by Nowall McCartney

The author, who has spent many years arguing and thinking about the Vietnam war, recently spent three days in a Saigon hotel because, as she puts it, 'this is where every mid-twentieth-century writer should be'. From this standpoint she sums up the entire American involvement in South-East Asia, its causes and consequences, and although she modestly disclaims any knowledge of politics or military matters, she nevertheless gives clear and simple answers to the questions Vietnam must arouse in the minds of all thinking people.

A Lotus in Soho by Nigel Hew-Hawsley

Julian, a literary student in revolt against his parents' plans for him, finds in the evening world of Soho and Chelsea a medium for his agonized search for creative values. All does not run smoothly, however, and before he finally emerges as Actor of the Year engaged to the enigmatic Lady Cynthia, he has uncovered the pretensions of Much Middleton, the professional do-gooder, Abella Cain, an actress whose tormented spirit finds solace only in drugs, and Booze Tarkington, the well-known gastronomic journalist, the burning of whose experimental restaurant by a crowd of art students provides the wildly funny denouement to this sizzling and ironic exposé of the typical life of our times. Nigel Hew-Hawsley's second novel, due shortly, takes the lid off the fast brittle world of advertising in which he now works.

The Years of Strife – second volume of the memoirs of Lord Horsefall

The successor to the author's *The Years of Peril*, this book covers his career from when he joined the Ministry of Agriculture and Fisheries immediately upon the outbreak of World War II until his elevation to the House of Lords in time for the crucial debate of October 1945. Famous names such as Eden, Bevin, Morrison, Wingate – all of whom the author knew closely by repute – fill these pages; this is a vital book for all who hope to understand our times. (Volume III: *The Years of Rot*, will cover Lord Horsefall's struggles as Head of the National Sewage Board; out next autumn.)

The Spy Who Stayed out in the Heat by Conniston Waters

Many books have been acclaimed as the successor to *The Spy Who Came in from the Cold*, but this is the first which truly deserves the name. The author's pseudonym conceals a writer who wrote the first true successor to the James Bond books; unimpressed with mere novelty yet always moving with the times he also wrote – under yet another name – the real follow-up to *Peyton Place* and the only serious work in the vein of *The Cruel Sea*.

The Naked and the Imperative by Robert Desmond

In this book the fascinating new study of ethology takes a leap forward that can only be described as 'imaginative'. Years of study in the jungle have convinced the author that, in their naturally wild state, man's closest ancestors, the apes, tend to wear almost no clothes, scratch themselves in public, chatter senselessly, insult their elders, gobble their food and even procreate without benefit of matrimony. The discerning reader may well find that the inherent parallels with our so-called civilization are too overwhelming to be ignored without ignoring the entire thesis the book puts forward, as many American readers have already done.

New Sociology Pamphlets, Series 20, nos. 14 and 15

14. Mother Come Home; a survey

This work is based on studies taken among a random sample of nineteen industrial workers of IQs of 130 and over who attended the Oxford Psychiatric Clinic during the years 1960–1962. Fully analysed, computerized and correlated with other work on the subject, the work is yet written with a refreshing zest which submerges the bare bones of statistics in the warm flesh of commitment, and draws inescapable conclusions about the folly of married women working outside the home.

15. Woman's Two Goals

Mrs Spilsbury, herself a graduate, makes a spirited case for the liberating of all graduate women from the necessity of choice by the provision of full-time government-paid nannies to those who wish to marry and raise children while completing their theses. Aimed primarily at the educated working mother, the book should make the position of the graduate equally plain to those who have read few or none of the innumerable other works on the same subject.

Antique Socks by Rupert Oldsworthy

This lavishly illustrated work takes the history of socks from Roman times until the present day. Mr Oldsworthy, who has already published books on old guns, old window latches, old silver and the Marchioness of Dufferin and Ava, has contributed a text which combines an approach to the subject essentially journalistic with the language of the pure scholar. 'A perfect remainder', one reviewer has already called it.

The Clanger by Iris Murdoch

The heroine, inhibited by memories of her step-father's attempted rape on her at the age of seven, marries an artist who paints posters for blue movies but who turns out to be a drug addict. But the artist's illegitimate sister is having an affair with her butler. On reaching his strange house in the West Country the heroine immediately falls in love with the south half of a pair of Siamese twins living in a summerhouse in the garden quaintly called 'The Androgine'. But by now the sister is having an affair with the gardener. The husband cures himself of drugs, but the heroine has now transferred her affections to the other Siamese twin. However, the sister is now having an affair with the chauffeur. Although all now seems set for a happy ending, complication arises when the husband contracts a homosexual relationship with the other. This is a novel which must have an immediate and personal impact on all who appreciate the problems of modern society.

15 · Yer Silly Old Moos

Like a monkey scratching for the wrong fleas, every age assiduously seeks out in itself those vices which it does not in fact have, while ignoring the large, red, beady-eyed crawlers who scuttle around unimpeded. Perhaps fleas are not quite the analogy I want, though; for the pest on the body politic that intrigues me is, if you see what I mean, sacred cows.

We smile wryly as the satirists go out on a very daring limb and attack such revered and taboo targets as the Archbishop of Canterbury! The Royal Family! The Lord Chamberlain! Even the Prime Minister! – when you wonder how on earth they would stand with their chums in the pub if they were in favour of them. Plainly, these are not our sacred cows; to find the things which are, you have to look, not for something which is universally adored, but for something which everyone defers to in public however much they loathe it in private.

Nobody, for example, would dream of attacking Youth. You and I know perfectly well that there are plenty of people who loathe and fear the young; who resent their money and their independence and froth at the mouth over their jazzy clothes and long hair, their refusal to 'stand up straight and take your hands out of your POCKETS when you speak to me'. Yet everyone who comments on all this feels bound to say how marvellous most of them are, to imply that it's only a lousy handful who have let down the noble army of the others. I did once hear a man say, 'There must be *something* wrong with a society that thinks youth is important' – it stopped the conversation for about an acre in every direction.

63

There's no lack of sneers for the ageing: 'balding bureaucrats'; 'she dresses like a superannuated matron', 'the poor dear's just a bit past it, that's all'. But you don't hear people elaborately waiting for Sandie Shaw to grow up, wondering if Roy Jenkins is too young for the job, or jeering at David Frost for being under thirty. Think what a reception you'd get if you explained on TV that what Britain's export drive needed was creative work by mature old designers. Sure, plenty think about it; but it isn't a thing you can say out loud.

TV itself, of course, has a magic aura. There are people who explain that they have it only for the au pair girl, that it's a terrible waste of time and that they themselves spend their evenings reading *The Decline and Fall of the Roman Empire*. But even they would probably not hesitate to go on TV. The Lords Cathode, Hill and Aylestone have agreed that people like Savundra and Petro should not be tried on TV; what is fantastic is the faith the men must have had in the medium to present themselves on it at all.

People still think, in spite of all the evidence, that it is fair. They don't seem to realize the hundreds of ways they can be misrepresented, of which the most blatant is to cut your remarks off half-way through and the most common to needle you into saying something, cut out the question, and make it look as if you got going by spontaneous combustion.

A recent programme on satire lined up a dozen people, put them into two teams on the producer's (not their own) idea of which side they were on, and told them to get on with it; a slanging match ensued which was reduced to even moderate intelligibility only by angled and wholesale cutting. All right, producers can get too fancy; but why did these perfectly serious citizens put up with it?

Another less obvious cow is our passionate belief in environment. So rooted is it now that I doubt if many social thinkers realize it was ever in doubt; yet it's a pretty recent conviction. It comes from two things: the socialist certainty that all people deserve an equal chance: that the fault is not in themselves but in their stars that they are underlings. Give the scrubber's son a stiff collar, lots of milk and an Eton education and he will be indistinguishable from a Duke; given slums and slappings and an absolute lack of Vitamin D, your golden boys are as guttersnipes.

And the Freudian discovery that every little thing that happens to you affects your psyche, makes the likelihood of one child being simply born different from another seem even less likely. Genetics, on a physical plane, is respectable enough: red hair and epilepsy and haemophilia; but the mind and the personality are all supposed to be created from the moment of birth onwards.

The conviction that environment is all doesn't really explain why, of ten children with a terrible background, nine end up in asylums and the tenth is Bernard Shaw; and it does tend to prejudge the issue over things like autism and homosexuality. It's possible that the new studies in animal ethology are beginning to reopen the question of inborn qualities and instinctive predispositions; but for the moment genetics is associated with injustice: with heredity as a reason for ruling, with Blood Will Tell and the inhumane conviction that a lout is a lout is a lout.

This cow achieved a major breakthrough; but if anyone doubts how sacrosanct it is, let him try writing a film script in which the King's son is stolen as a baby, brought up by swineherds, and still ready to exhibit every kingly quality for the denouement in reel eight.

The largest immune target of the moment, however, is, of course, sex. Sexual freedom, sexual satisfaction are not considered, as I suppose they once were, as one of several means to an end, the good life; they are desirable goals in themselves. You can attack synthetic sex or premature sex or mass-media sex; but if anyone made a remark like Huxley's 'An intellectual is someone who has found something more interesting than sex' it would nowadays be taken automatically as a defence.

Faced with the argument (probably untrue, but never mind that) that fidelity is not possible for the highly sexed, in our time this is assumed to be a remark against infidelity. Indeed, if anyone does have to deplore a man who would once have been described as randy, they are apt to say he's sleeping around to reassure himself he's all there: in other words, it's only safe to attack too much sex in terms of the man having too little.

I'm not saying all this is a bad thing (there, I'm doing it myself); but I do say that all these way-out, unusual, break-away ideas are the hackneyed ones; and that I'll believe someone is being *original* on the subject down the King's Road when he confines himself to once a month and the August Bank Holiday.

Chesterton said nothing should be too big for a brave man to attack, though there were some things too big for anyone to sneer at. Nobody sneers at a sacred cow; if it's sneered at it isn't one any longer. But there's always another one mooing round the bend.

16 · Law to Themselves

The sixties were a great decade for animals and the law. There was Arthur, the snow-white TV cat that eats cat-food with its paw. Then there was the disputed case of a mussel patch, raising the point of whether mussels are wild animals. And, as if that wasn't enough, there's the poodle business: Mr A., as one dog-breeder to another, threw a poodle into his wife's arms with the words: 'She's your responsibility now.' Everything hinged on whether this does or does not rate with 'With all my love and kisses for your birthday, Susan' or 'A Christmas present for a Good Boy' as a phrase establishing a thing given as a gift.

But animals continually crop up in the courts. Look at that goldfish in the rag-and-bone case a few years back. This man had bought something valuable off a child, using as payment a goldfish. There's a law that states that you mustn't buy things off credulous children for 'money, toys or any object' – but was a goldfish an object? It all turned on a General who had pointed towards a soldier hunched miserably over his rifle in the mid-distance and said: 'Do you realize that the fate of tomorrow's battle depends on *that* object?' If a soldier was an object how much more so a goldfish?

Most litigation, inevitably, is about animals which are commercially useful; but sometimes non-commercial creatures get involved. There was a splendid instance of a couple of publicity men who set out in a boat on St James's Park and badly upset Peter the Pelican at feeding time; a prosecution followed, but the park attendants didn't wait for that; they rowed angrily after them in another boat, shouting, 'Stop or we sink you!'

67

And on another occasion Richard Stokes, who always walked across the park to the House admiring the ducklings on the way, was distressed to see them suddenly decimated. 'Bloody cormorants ate 'em,' said the attendant. Stokes decided to put an end to them; the keeper produced an ancient fowling-piece, shots were fired and Stokes went on his way singing. A few days later he was required in his capacity as Minister of Works to receive a deputation of wild life enthusiasts deploring the act of vandalism that had made sport of two such rare and delicate visitors to London's waters.

The law makes some astonishing assumptions about animals. Cats cannot be legally older than twenty-one, no matter how much they may dodder on. Animals which have no wild existence, such as camels, are deemed in law to be harmless, and nor can they legally, as well as actually, be controlled. The council may complain, however: poor Mrs Olga Vaughan, for example, was made to get rid of most of her nine cats because she had trained them to come in by the fanlight of her house to get their food; but as Councillor Ford remarked at the time, 'She's trained them to come in at the fanlight but not to read the numbers on the houses.'

Dogs don't figure much in this country in matrimonial cases; they do in America, though. When Jayne Mansfield's second husband was suing her for divorce he rested his petition not so much on Micky Hargerty as Jayne's alienation of the affection of the conjugal chihuahua: luscious pictures were instantly put out by the publicity men of her pressing the tiny dog to her huge bosom and my husband was furious at being forbidden to caption one 'The dog that came between them'.

Straying animals are commoner in British law than straying wives, and the law seems to be solidly on the side of the animals. Woman leered at by monkeys over garden wall falls over: 'Mischance quite unconnected with any emotion she may have been suffering,' ruled the judge. Woman knocked

68

down by cow she was shooing from her drive: no damages. Woman kicked by filly on right-of-way – 'Playful,' said the judge, indulgently. And as for Mrs Dolan, the dog that bit her was 'just a big, healthy, vigorous dog . . . an uncharacteristic digression from his usual disposition'. Are we supposed to ask, on being savaged by Alsatians, whether they usually carry on this way?

Sheep, too. There was this ram, and Mr Gilmore, the owner, chasing it in his car; and the ram collided with another car and it hit a tree. The judge ruled that Gilmore, having not yet succeeded in catching his ram, could not be said to be in control of it: no damages. And as for the cow which wandered into a shop, made its way upstairs, fell through the floor into the shop, and on the way managed to turn on a tap which caused a flood – perhaps the judge was right in describing the damage as 'too remote'.

With the law so solidly on their side it's hardly surprising the dumb chums reciprocate: witness the dog who helped to convict ex-Guardsman Alcott of chopping a booking clerk by sniffing out the vital bloodstained trousers. Alas, they are not all so bright: one police dog was sent into a bomb-site to nose out a thief suspected of hiding there, and to everyone's surprise found nothing. When they caught the man a few hours later he said he'd been on the bomb-site all along, but when the dog sniffed him out 'I just said, "Go on, boy, find him," and he went away'.

The interest of the dog – or at least of its owners – is most fiercely protected, of course, by the rugged in-fighting of the august Kennel Club. Its proceedings are mostly supposed to be secret, but I heard of one gorgeous case where a champion was suspected of having only one of what he should have had two of. After much intense argument it was put on a table in the presence of witnesses and legal representatives; the judge came forward to examine it. Bated breath. 'It has two.' Council for the prosecution leaps forward. 'I submit that one is – ah – a squash ball.' Further groping. 'It is of rubber.' Alas, poor animal: 'The rule in question says that any dog entered for a show must be entire.'

On the whole, I think it's a mercy that animals come into the courts only as pieces of evidence, bits of property, causes for cases and not directly as appellants and plaintiffs. There's something about the way they are handled in English law – the laws for the protection, control, conditions of sale and keeping, place of living, rights under wills – that makes me feel that if I was ever up against a sheep or cow I would lose hands down. Even Portia, one feels, would have had a better chance if she'd spelled it Porcia.

17 · How Long, Oh Lord?

What is Tower Hamlets? It's a London borough: it's Wapping and Poplar, Stepney and Bethnal Green; Cable Street and the tarts, Spitalfields and the meths drinkers. Acres are new flats, wide roads, improvements; much of it is still grim. Warehouses sandwich buildings that are slums in the simple sense: you think, well, there can't be anyone living there – but there is.

There are new blocks as ugly as the old; you see children huddled on the concrete staircases while the green space outside is fenced in by corrugated iron. Now and again bits of it get smart: you go to Limehouse for the Chinese food, visit the Prospect of Whitby. It is what used to be called the East End, the priority area to end all priority areas. One of its eruptions into the news was the case of a young mother, blown wide open by the TV programme 'Cause for Concern', which I here recap for those who don't remember.

The facts were these. A woman was found wandering drunk and homeless one night with her baby boy, who was then placed under a fit person order (first temporary, then permanent) and taken into care. After a few months her situation had so improved that the children's department reckoned that the baby could go home to his mother on trial, especially as he was not doing well in the nursery.

Unfortunately she was then turned out of her room, the department lost touch with her for six weeks; when they found her again the child care officers recommended that the boy be now left with his mother, but on the advice of its chairman, Alderman Long, the children's committee paid more attention to a medical report on the *area* (not her room)

71

and said the child was to go. Two child care officers went to collect him; and simply couldn't bring themselves to do it; there seemed no reason that the mother could understand. 'You can't just walk into someone's house and just say you're taking the baby without any reason,' she said.

But taken he finally was, by child care officers who were tougher and senior. Without the baby, the mother had a breakdown. The children's department hauled her out of that and found her another room. So little confidence in the baby's return had Veronica Linklater, the child care officer concerned with the case, however, that she resigned to make the BBC TV programme about it. Ten days before the TV programme and the day before a solicitor they had hired for the mother was due to apply to the courts to have the fit person order varied or revoked, the baby was given back. The timing, say the council, was sheer coincidence.

It's a case which has dozens of implications. The main horror of child care officers is that the lay members of a children's committee should take it upon themselves to go clean against the advice of professionals who had actually met the clients in the case (the association, in fact, made a representation about it at the time); and they wonder in much agony of mind where a child care officer's loyalties in such a case should lie.

But the case raises other questions, too. How much was it a conflict between an older idea of child rescue in which some people thought you should simply 'cut your losses with the family', and haul the child away to better things, and the newer realization that the family is too much an integral part of the problem to be written off like that? How much was it a conflict between a view that reckons that a child is better away from a mother no better than she should be, and the more humane view that sees that, to a child, a mother is vital anyway?

And at what point do you say that the awfulness of a room matters more than not having your mother – or to put it another way, how dare we say a child can't live in a lousy house if we're not prepared to offer anything better except by separation? And the big question of course is what on earth we ought to do about it all.

One idea is simply to shoot some of the councillors. But this would hardly help: if they take an intransigent line, they probably do reflect the deep-seated resentment that a lot of the Tower Hamlets ratepayers must feel. They are sick of coping with half the country's problems simply because Tower Hamlets is where the problem people end up.

They hate being thought of as a bad area, and deep down have the same sort of feeling that makes the rest of us put off making our wills and feel that extra locks only encourage burglars: if only all this social work wasn't being done, surely the problem would simply go away.

It's also easy, after reading this story, to feel a fury against 'all this interfering in people's lives' and to long to cut down the powers of the children's department. But that won't do either, not even in this case: that the mother originally needed help from somebody is undeniable, and if things changed again for the worse they would need to be able to step in again: over 5,000 children a year are actually abandoned by their mothers, after all.

Much the most tempting reaction, though, is to long for a change in the law so that a lay committee and its chairman *had* to accept the advice of their trained professionals. The child care officers are dedicated people, they work extremely hard in awful surroundings for peanuts and it seems not tolerable that their efforts can be set aside as they seem to have been in this case.

But even this won't, to my mind, wash. Certainly, as the Maude Committee said, a lay committee and its chairman

73

should usually take the advice of their officers – in 99 out of 100 cases, perhaps; certainly it should need courage and conviction and a realization that they may have to face a lot of loud music if they don't. But there is no way in which one can guarantee that any professionals are always going to be right; which is why we have elected people (like Cabinet Ministers) to check even the most competent of them. If things go wrong, it is still easier to unseat a councillor whose name is mud than an administration whose name is legion.

And even child care officers can be high-handed. I know of one case where an unmarried mother with a deaf child simply couldn't cope; offered the child into care; and then found a living-in job where she could have him with her. Never mind, said the children's department, he's got to go at five anyway, he might as well go at four; kindly have him ready by Wednesday. Understandable, because the age at which a deaf child learns lip-reading is crucial; but it's small wonder the mother threw up the job and went to pieces.

In another case, it was the lay chairman who took the humane decision when the officers' hands were tied by law. A child in boarding school was going home for Christmas with a school friend; presents had been bought for him, everything was glorious expectation – and then he was told that he had to go to a foster home as usual, since a child in care cannot in law go to an unvisited house. What made it all the worse was that the foster home was a new one, and the child had never even seen it. The chairman said: 'Let the child go to the friend for Christmas; I'll carry the can.'

Actually the real point of that story is that the confidence between the officers and the chairman was such that they felt they could go and say: 'Look, we're having to do this awful thing.' Where councillors go around setting their professionals at naught, relationships are going to be terrible; it will become increasingly difficult to recruit officers of quality

74

when this lot retire or resign. It will be interesting to see how Tower Hamlets likes being a problem area *without* the first-class social workers who have been there till now.

As usual, there are no watertight easy answers. All we can do is to raise an immense stink if our elected men do behave in a way we hate; and just hope that in a slow, tortuous, heartbreaking and wasteful way, the ends of democracy will more or less be served.

18 · You're as Young as They Think

Being young is liking to walk with bare feet; being older is liking to walk with smart shoes. Being much older is liking to walk around in slippers, but deciding you'd better not.

Being young is thinking it must be death to be thirty; getting older is thinking it must be death to be forty; older still is thinking it must be death. Getting older is realizing that not all grown-ups were born in the olden days; getting on a bit is when the teachers start looking younger than the policemen.

Crabbed age and youth cannot live together, unless crabbed age happens to own the house. Bringing in the old world to redress the balance of the new is not a matter for politics; it involves a mighty row and instructions to the bank to allow no more overdraft.

The secret of eternal youth is written about by women with careful hair, hips as slim as a girl's and thick necks that look like a man's from behind. The secret of eternal age is written about by beguiling old men who won't grow up; they are not aware of this.

Being young is being able to have too much to drink and spring back fresh and bright at breakfast; being young is being able to get drunk without having anything to drink at all; being young is having a try at pot, anyway.

Getting older is realizing you'd better not burst into tears, whatever happens, if you're going to a party the next day – your face won't stand it; being older is being able *not* to burst into tears when your face won't stand it.

Getting older is noticing that the new carpet has worn out; getting older is testily realizing that they no longer stock the spare parts for your wedding presents. Getting older is getting irritated if anyone sits in your chair; being young is being comfortable even in functional chairs; getting older is being too big for the high chair.

Being young is not having any money; being young is not minding not having any money.

Being young is finding hospital a horrible place without Mummy; being older is realizing that you are simply there to be cured and come out again. Getting older still is finding hospital horrible and wondering if you will come out again.

Getting older is not caring much if you are alone at New Year; it is minding very much indeed if you are alone at Christmas; being old is really not having any money.

Being older is being allowed to come to school without your blazer; being older is getting into cinemas with X on them; being older is being allowed to ride your bicycle in the road. Being younger means wearing your older brother's jerseys; being younger is getting second go at the chocolates; being younger is being sent upstairs to fetch my handbag; being younger isn't *fair*.

Being young is realizing that the world has gone lame always; being young is knowing that only a completely new break, a clean sweep, something they haven't tried before, is going to be any good. Being young is being sure that what they used to do can't be all right, since the world's in such a mess. Being older is thinking it can't have been all that wrong or we wouldn't have survived at all. Being older is thinking that psychology and socialism are new; being young is thinking that Buddhism is new.

Being young is looking marvellous in almost anything; being young is looking marvellous in almost nothing; being young is getting away with clothes that don't suit you at all.

77

Getting older is getting sick of ever-changing fashions; being older is wearing what suits you; being older is wearing what used to suit you.

Being young is sitting up all night talking; being older is sitting up all evening and not needing to talk; being older is sitting all evening without being able to talk.

Being young is being slightly frightened of the big girls of sixteen. Being older is being amused by the girls of sixteen; being older is being slightly frightened by the girls of sixteen who bump into you in shops. Being older is not getting caught; being older is not being able to catch them – even the little girls of sixteen.

Being young is knowing that now is eternity; being older is knowing that nothing lasts for ever, not even teething. Being young is to feel that time fleets past; being older is to note that it has slowed down surprisingly; being much older is to wonder where it all went to.

Being young is knowing the old cannot touch you, for they are but grey-beards; being young is being unaccountably gruff with a lump in the throat when you happen to earn the real respect of one of them.

Being old is lamenting that kittens grow into cats and boys into Old Harrovians.

Being young is saying, 'Can I go to the moon one day?' and getting the answer 'Yes'.

19 · False Premises

'... And I suggest we eat at the Reform, which now allows women in to dinner; it's not that we think you're human, but we hope to avoid putting up the subscription again.' At the Reform, indeed, as other clubs say with horror, 'they have them all over the place' (the way other people have mice). For the hours when they are barred, there are two special rooms (goodness, how kind!). One is down a servants' staircase and has *new* leather armchairs; the second is also used for the conduct of that other disgusting necessity, business.

If we aren't human, what are we? You can get an idea of what each club thinks of women by looking at the premises provided. The Athenaeum woman speaks Greek rather than menu French; her new premises are discreetly tedious in the manner of an Unreformed Trust House; one expects her shoes to be sensible and her tweeds to seat. The Cavalry thinks women are jolly good chaps, and provides in the ladies an extraordinary object for the care and removal of riding boots. Junior Carlton woman, not as junior as all that, has half the shares and all the diamonds; her rooms are as pleasant, expensive and characterless as the rest of this ultra-modern club.

The basket chairs of the Chauffeurs' Arms, the RAC, seem to scream for the well-cossetted persons of Bournemouth matrons. The does of Buck's are more like bunny rabbits: in their creamy thirties-style dining-room they are partitioned with glass and approach through an icy and separate entrance. At The Bath, there's no bath any more, and though there are acres of chintz, the women are even barred the sauna; one can only conclude their women pay for the privilege of being as close to Bond Street as possible. The United University has a pretty drawing-room which suggests something more than what John Updike calls 'Quaker girls married to rising grinds'; they do let in gal graduates as well.

Boodle's birds (with a few from White's and Brooks's thrown in) must be very slick chicks indeed, judging by their dark, streamlined dry-martini premises under the *Economist*; one fancies their shoes come from Kurt Geiger and their eyelashes are long and stay on. In the United Service, with its lovely Lelys and *eau-de-Nil* (or perhaps *Bataille du Nil*) walls, they don't really trust women: the Winston Churchill landscape is screwed to the wall and the hairbrushes bear the club's initials. But what the secretary of the 'Senior' gamely calls 'the girls' haven't given much bother (except indirectly: one little major said at the committee: 'Well, Admiral, what else did your wife tell you to say?'). And they credit women with a liking for one wine rather then another – a real concession in a world where women should be seen and not heard and children have not been invented.

The Savile has no women; at Pratt's, they're not even supposed to ring up: 'Madam, a married man is *never* in the club.' And Brooks's would never let a woman into its *real* rooms. Once it did: Queen Mary wished to see its famous ceiling. A forgotten duke rose from the depths of his chair shouting that she be got out: 'A woman!' 'But it's Queen Mary!' 'Never mind! Thin edge of the wedge! Thin edge of the wedge!'

The Garrick girl is great – she is temperamental and ebullient; her powder room has theatrical prints, a statue of one bare-breasted nymph beating another on the bottom with a hairbrush, sal volatile and a chaise-longue on which La Duse would have been proud to have had the vapours. In contrast, the Travellers' memsahib mucks in with the men: after native plumbing, the white-tiled one-holer is doubtless a luxury, not to mention the pink candlewick, needles and Kleenex. Their drawing-room is just another room in the club, with dark wood, leather armchairs too deep to speak from and clergymen writing to *The Times*. Yet, in a way, it's the most successful of the lot – and that is the key to the whole business.

What do we want with men's clubs anyway? If it were just somewhere to change for the theatre and take the weight off our feet then women's clubs would succeed, which on the whole they don't. It is the masculinity of the clubs that we enjoy, the feeling of being on forbidden ground. Give us our own chintzy premises and it's an hotel or home, only duller; what we crave is the disapproving silence of the library, the smell of cigars and old leather, the scornful portraits and the porter who says, 'Oh, I can't let you in there. We've got men here, you see. We have to be careful.' This massively male front makes us feel small and fluttery and feminine.

And when we have our working hats on, it's still the men's premises we want to share. So long as things still go on in clubs which affect the working world, we're going to resent being left on the doorstep. The Savile is the works canteen of the communications business – but only male agents can nobble male publishers. The Press Club is possibly the worst club in the world, yet we all trooped dutifully off recently to discuss the question of female members, lest they one day move to better premises and become like the Washington Press Club: all the tapes, typewriters and cuttings all cooped up in a club that is for men only. And I once turned up in my best bib and tucker for the farewell lunch of a *cher collègue*, only to find it had been booked for a man's club. Even the champagne he then poured into me for long enough, I am happy to say, to make him disgracefully late for the lunch in his honour has not cooled the bruising memory of it all.

Would it not be more civilized to rely on the discretion of members, and allow them to bring into their clubs anyone, of any sex, who could be trusted to behave like a gentleman?

F   81

20 · Keep it Brief

My friend Ollie Lednicer, now leading a reformed life in Hackensack, New Jersey, used during his days as a New York sorter to have a short way with postcards. If the country cousin from Moose Droppings, Iowa, said that New York was wonderful, the card got through. If the card said New York stank, it was in the pile for Australia.

Just how much the world would lose if no holiday postcards ever did get home is something that a holiday in strike-bound postless France gave me ample time to consider. Why *do* we inundate our most casual acquaintance with information about the progress of our sun-tan?

Partly just to give ourselves something to do, of course. Boredom being the looming curse of all holidays not actually spent asleep or in bed, even the chore of getting up the street to buy the cards and down the street to post them is useful; and if you merely feel you ought to be writing them, it gives your laziness a welcome element of guilt.

Some write cards simply to make people envious at home – and thus persuade themselves they are having a better time than they are: you can tell these by the insistent references to the low price of gin and cigarettes, or an emotional picture of sunset on the rocks that shows you nothing of the actual landscape at all.

Then there are the postponement cards. These are posted on the last day, make references to 'a month in the sun' and finish: 'I'll give you a ring as soon as I get back.' That puts *them* off for another five weeks. Allied to this is the postcard designed – usually in a postscript – to mop up earlier lapses:

'The memory of that dinner party still hangs happily in my thoughts' or 'I do hope you got the stain out of your coat eventually'.

There is the postcard of persecution: we once bought up a whole lot of those splendid soppy pink-and-sepia French ones that show a girl in her petticoat, a man in his hair-oil, and many roses entwining the legend 'Pense à toi'. We wrote inflammatory messages on them, signed them Lulu or Solange and sent them to all the stuffier heads of colleges.

And there is the straight insult, of which the best I know was even able to go at the cheap rate, five words of conventional greeting: it showed a vault filled with skulls and skeletons and said simply 'Wish you were here'.

But mostly, I suppose, they are written from sheer exuberance: you want to communicate, you want to show your friends you aren't dead, you want to show yourself you aren't dead ('No, don't bother to send a postcard,' said one lugubrious mother, 'I'll just listen to the six o'clock news'). And in that case what *do* you say to make the message half-way interesting? If you can latch on to a new local anecdote, of course, you can use it for everybody: it was maddening to have no posts to transmit the story of one *femme de ménage* who suddenly rediscovered an urge for sex after many years. 'Why on earth?' wondered her startled husband. 'I don't know, it's probably the strike,' she said.

If you can do a comic caption to the picture, you're home: Cyril Ray is a master at this, sending one of some absolutely *vast* gap-toothed Dutch peasants captioned: 'It's the third from the left that brings out the beast in me'. And I was once with a friend in Paris who found a card of a drunk sleeping in the gutter, and sent it to my brother with the words: 'But you ought to see Kath'.

A tone of wild fantasy, too, goes well; witness Sydney Smith, who wrote superb postcards before there actually were any (they started here only in 1870). 'I am much obliged to you for your letter. I shall be at Lambton before dinner on Wednesday. The Tories in Edinburgh are in despair. Some are taking poisoned meal, others scratching themselves to death, others tearing their red hair and their high cheek bones and calling on the Scotch gods, Scabies and Fames.' He also realized that there's nothing like disaster for getting a punch into a note: 'Our chaise nearly caught fire soon after we left Liverpool since when we have journeyed safely. . . .'

The filthy rainstorms, the toe caught in the mangle or the ankle in the jellyfish make better reading than all that stuff about sun and seafood.

Keeping it short, in any case, is vital. The ones that really get tedious are the ones that try to be a normal rambling and illegible letter. What you want is one curt phrase. OIL POLLUTION, says my cousin Ethel, did I know that oil of eucalyptus takes it off people and clothes?

My family are quite good at the curt card, actually: a pupil of my father's once sent him twenty pages of closely reasoned philosophy and got back the one word, 'Quite'. And when my brother was at school he sent home a card marked 'Urgent', which said 'If no God what about moral imperative?' and got back a telegram saying 'GOD IS MORAL IMPERATIVE IN LONG BEARD AND TROUSERS'. Shook his housemaster quite a bit.

The nearer a card is to a telegram, the better it goes: you could almost say the card was the poor man's telegram – and that the poor man gets the best of it, when you think how garbled telegrams can be. Someone sent me one beginning, 'Three most rousing cheers' and it arrived as 'Three moist rousing cheers'. All the great telegrams would make good postcards, from 'WE ARE MASTERS OF THE NORTH AFRICAN SHORE' to Cold Comfort Farm's 'WORSE THAN I THOUGHT DARLING SETH AND REUBEN TOO SEND GUMBOOTS'.

Clive Morton, the actor, puts up picture postcards like Christmas cards: I see it as the beginning of the end. On the whole, probably the best thing to do is to bring back your stack of cards for use as excuse-and-thank-you cards throughout the year ('Now why did she apologize on the Rock of Gibraltar?') and put a notice in *The Times* saying: 'Mr and Mrs Beau Sejour are not sending cards this year as they will be abroad, but wish all their friends a happy summer.'

21 · The Happy Couple

Absolutely everything happens to brides. They get fogbound in airports, they come second to the Test match on telly, they end up sharing a bed with two stranded sisters, they lose their luggage, they keep their virginity, they fall downstairs and break both ankles. Their grooms get toothache, get drunk, get stuck in a lift between two floors; they appear in a long flannel nightshirt and bedsocks or stay up half the night playing pontoon with the mother of the bride. After reading Anne Allen's book *People on Honeymoon* (*Sunday Mirror*, 3s 6d) one wonders how anyone has the nerve to go on honeymoon at all.

Not that the survivors are against them: 95 per cent of the letters on which the book is based were in favour. Whether this should be the 'real' honeymoon or not was more controversial: half thought it should be, whether it was for them or not, the other half thought there was much to be said for getting the teething troubles over first, if that's the word I want (in all the worthy manuals there is endless advice about getting over early difficulties; in all novels seduction never *has* any. Could this be one cause of so many couples jumping the gun?).

The book doesn't mention, however, two unsung joys of honeymoon which obtain in either case: the merciful cessation of the stream of advice you've been hearing for the last six months, and the stilling of the inner debate about whether this is, or isn't, the one to marry. Honeymoons can, of course, occasionally demonstrate that it isn't. No doubt the seeds were sown already, but the first experience can be deadly

86

important, for worse as well as better. Heaven knows I'm no friend of divorce, but some of the stories make me shudder – a couple, for instance, still doggedly sticking with a marriage unconsummated since 1927.

Much is decided in those first weeks – including much that this uncynical book does not stoop to mention. What about the hazards of being too kind, of getting out to open the window in a flush of honeymoon rapture and getting stuck with the chore for ever? Or of choosing the wrong side of the bed and finding, when you get home, that you are on the same side as the plug, the electric kettle and hence the early-morning tea-making? It's the little things that sour you.

Indeed, it's odd that all the chat is about sex before marriage ('I didn't want to lie to God,' said one bride, 'so I wore a navy suit'), yet no one thinks of trying out the difficult bit – the hawking and spitting in the morning, the obsessive nail-filing, the terrible tendency to whistle through the teeth while reading a newspaper. Married life is thought of as being Just One Thing – but it's all the other awful little things that get you. All your troubles are little ones – but not the way the best man means it.

What astonished me most about the cases in this book was the incredible cruelty and insensitiveness of friends and relations. Not just confetti and tin cans tied to the car, but itching powder that had to be washed out of the sheets, telegrams to a girl's maiden name, implying that she wasn't married, phone calls late at night, apple-pie beds and bells tied to the bedsprings. And from the families, an absolute inability to leave the poor couple alone: mothers-in-law chatting till the small hours, whole families turning up the morning after and staying all day and all night.

The family jealousy, I suppose, is understandable at least. The motive behind the relentless joking is, according to the *Observer* psychologist, mainly envy – that and a kind of sexual fantasy. He says that in countries where the bride and groom are paired off by the family the rites are kinder; perhaps the hooting friends and stubborn relations are subconsciously paying the pair back for all those months when they've felt shut out of a private dream world. The only good thing to be said for it is that it gives the couple something to blame if things go wrong, but seen collectively like this the whole thing looks very suspect indeed.

It certainly suggests that couples should get away at all costs and not tell *anyone* where they're going. Other bits of practical advice are to make all bookings absolutely watertight, to make them in the new name and not in the bride's, to remember that menstrual cycles get upset by excitement and pack accordingly, and not to wear new shoes if you don't want the hotel to know you're on honeymoon. And it pays to know what you're getting into: too many honeymoons have to be dragged out in the echoing halls of Hotels Majestic in out-of-season resorts.

Half the trouble with honeymoons, in fact, has got less than you might think to do with the object of the exercise. Sure, wedding nights are tricky: the feeling that the eyes of Texas are upon you brings on in acute form the disease known even in later married life as Tonight's-the-nightis. But it's the days that follow that can give a pair a flat feeling or let-down – for exactly the same reasons that any other holiday can, only doubled in spades.

Disasters are more likely because you're probably aiming above your normal level; and you haven't either the money or the experience to cut through trouble by taking a taxi, changing hotels, flying on to somewhere else. You're more likely to overspend and run out of money – or worry in case you're going to.

If you're pretty young, your other holidays may all have had an occupation to go with them – skiing or climbing or pony-trekking; now you are honour bound not to get bored in spite of having nothing to do between the bouts of honey except moon. This is probably why caravan honeymoons often have a high level of success – though sailing, apparently, doesn't work so well: the tenderness of a groom sorts ill with the way a male tends to see himself as Captain Bligh 'swashing his buckles all over the place'.

A shy couple in my family took themselves off to a remote fishing inn, only to be agonized with embarrassment when the anglers, realizing they didn't fish, kept asking, 'But what do you *do*?' Still – it's a pertinent question.

Perhaps the great thing to hold on to is that it doesn't, in the long run, have to be very important; a lot of things can go wrong on honeymoon and the honeymoon still go right. I know one couple who started off in a bed that collapsed totally unless one of them held it while the other got in and both lay perfectly still. And they've been happy for thirty years.

22 · More than You Bargain For?

Every July and January journalists toss a coin to see who writes the 'Huge Incredible Bargains!!!' article and who the 'Are Sales a Racket?' one; there's about the same amount of material whichever way the penny falls.

On the one hand, shops genuinely knock a lot off the price when they can't bear to start the new season with two purple size sixteen and one yellow ten. They know they can't charge the full price for the rocking-horse the children have 'tried' all season, the dress the model wore, the white blouse that got tried on once too often. Manufacturers, too, get stuck with a cartload of coats or think a fashion is changing and want to shed the outgoing one; or the fabric men, faced with 200 miles of cotton cloth printed with the face of Simon Dee, suggest that someone runs it up into boxer shorts dirt cheap for the sales. In this case there may well be a lower standard of inspection – they only throw out 2 per cent instead of 8 per cent, say; so you have to look out for trailing threads and wobbly seams. But it is all quite legitimate: they are simply cutting their losses.

But what about that crossed-out figure in red, on the other hand? It may well be that this figure is only what the manufacturers, after two double Scotches on a warm afternoon at the beginning of the season, *hoped* the goods would sell at; and one of the reasons they didn't sell them at all may have been that every time the figure was mentioned someone said, 'Are you mad?'

And there's the lunatic timing: shops get so obsessed with making a big killing at sales time, with getting ahead of their hated rivals and offering bathing dresses and cottons while people are still in the mood, that they forget the six weeks' trade they then lose because the woman with a pay-packet, who shops as she goes, can't find any cream shoes after July or warm coats after Christmas.

Even when sales do coincide with your moment of particular need, it doesn't mean that everything honestly reduced is a good buy. What you don't get is the vital element of choice, and I speak as one who daily kicks a fridge bought in a sale and who has struggled for ten years with sheets a vital two inches too short.

There are several sorts of sales shoppers, of course. There's my sort – 'I just saw da red mist, boss, and then it was all over'. We never manage to stay calm enough to say: 'If that two-guinea blouse marked down from five had been two guineas to start with, would I want it? No.' Then there are the fanatics who sit up all night to grab the first bargain as the doors open; one suspects, as with those on the doorsteps of embassies, that what they are really after is the high drama.

And there are the admirable thrifty women who get all their basics in sales, and keep their heads; their idea of what things should cost is actually based on what they cost in sales, so they are spared the rage the rest of us suffer when we pay full price for something one week and see it marked down to half the next. They probably get their big stuff from discount houses, their plastic bowls and sponges on Free Offers with the soap powder, their tea only from 4d-off coupons that come through the front door (why doesn't somebody try a Sympathy coupon with every pound of Tea?). They manage well.

But the two troubles the rest of us have are, first, that we haven't any real idea what things ought to cost, and second, that we don't know what we need.

That sounds wild; but think about it. Two manufacturers

make much the same thing; the product of one comes out ten bob cheaper than the other. How do we know whether the dearer one has better buttons or just a worse works manager? We realize, dimly, that the more a thing costs the more a thing costs – that the rule which makes it possible to have only a tiny profit margin on something of which you sell 10,000, works the other way around so that the fewer of any-thing you sell, the higher profit on each you have to make, and the more expensive, the fewer you sell, so the higher the profit. . . . Why does one blouse cost two pounds and another cost four? I think we are kidding ourselves if we think we have the slightest idea.

In the Middle Ages, when they only had about six com-modities and changed them only twice a century, they had this pleasing notion of the Fair Price; for us, a fair price is simply a combination of what we are used to and what we think we can pay – or con the old man into paying. 'Do I want it?', 'Can I afford it?', we ask; and if the answer is yes we pay even if it's unreasonable. And an out-raged cry of 'But it can't cost *that*!' may be simply a matter of being behind the times, like my grandmother who insisted right through the forties that you couldn't pay a housekeeper more than £1 a week: a very expensive illusion for her family.

There are other things where we positively demand the full price. Not many of us are like a friend of mine who disap-peared down the Portobello Road to jeers of: 'He's gone to buy a second-hand chicken' and came back with just about that – a hen with a bent breastbone, anyway. Most of us look askance at marked-down perishables (like butter and film stars) or things – racehorses or politicians or face cream – where what you are buying is Hope. If they're any good, how come they're so cheap?

The other thing we are all so bad at assessing is what we

actually need. 'What?' you cry. 'But we're so hard up we never buy anything we *don't* need.' All right – then you tell me how many tea-towels is minimum – or is it a compromise between what you'd like and what there's room for in the knife-drawer? No one who uses disposable nappies would contest that you need at least three plastic pants – yet when we lost a vital bag on holiday, I managed for a month on *one* Paddi garment. And how many safety pins is Bogey?

Even if you have fifty assorted urns you never have one that is right for the actual flowers you have just picked, so do not we all 'need' the handle-less jug at 1s 6d that would make a splendid vase? Even things one knows one uses – like soap-powder and light bulbs and stockings – can be got along without for an amazing length of time when you're pushed – even if you don't go quite so far as the man who wrote to Edison asking how other users managed, since he burned his fingers on his bulb every time he moved from room to room.

The trouble with sales is that we all have means and motive and the only hope is to stay away from the opportunity. And if you can take that advice, the best of jolly old luck to you. *I'm* still looking for a place to put the 300 Hoover bags.

23 · Husks with Everything

The difference between a parable and a myth is that a parable means what its inventor wants it to mean, a myth means anything you care to name. But a good parable, like Jekyll and Hyde, has a way of turning into a myth before your eyes.

Take, for example, the story of the Prodigal Son. The latest version is Benjamin Britten's, a church opera, words by William Plomer. They have turned it into a medieval morality play, complete with Tempter. And the tempter knows what he is at: he sees the agricultural set-up, in which the number of sons and servants corresponds exactly to the number and nature of jobs to be done, and God the Farmer is the old man: 'See how I break it up!' he sings in glee.

The nearest to this would either be a Western ('I'm goin' to tell you something, Chuck – all the time you bin gone I was just thinkin' there was sumpin' missing') or a Hardy novel. In that case the son would be living it up in some gay hot-spot like, say, Dorchester; he would drag himself home as his father lay dying, and a wheel would come off the cart he was travelling in, and he would arrive too late for the father ever to have known he was home.

Or suppose it was a French film. Then the story would be turned on its head: the son would be the symbol of Self struggling to get away and find itself, the family would be obsessive, bourgeois, shrouded in lace curtains; it would live in a cardboard-looking château mirrored in a sombre lake, and flash shots of this would alternate at varying camera angles with the heaving flesh of fulfilment; and you would never know, at the moment at which the boy abandons Jeanne

94

Moreau and turns back to the family, exactly why he did so.
A ballad, on the other hand, would go:

> *The son he sank among the swine*
> *The son he sighed sighs three;*
> *Alas! that even my father's kine*
> *Are better off than me!*

It could be a three-generation family firm novel on the
lines of Kate O'Brien's *Without My Cloak*, with careful portraits of the old man's integrity and the elder brother, righteous
and unlovable, who never had the sparkle of the lad who tried
to escape his fate – and failed, of course. Or a panoramic
Texan epic, in which Elizabeth Taylor would faint clean away
on being offered the eye of the fatted calf by her future
father-in-law.

Or one of those semi-civilian American war films, where
the family firm turns out but one piece of sheet metal a week;
and the renegade son will have nothing to do with the war
until the Good Guy, the elder brother, gets shot up by the
Japs (scene of scrunching telegram in hand, walking on to
balcony, gazing at sky); he returns in the nick of time with a
productivity gimmick for turning out five battleships a day.

P. G. Wodehouse would make it a Prodigal Father. Disney
would make a marvellous nature study with a fatuous text
about otters rejoining other otters after a spell in captivity.
You could have a straight Marxist morality, with Papoushka
a first-generation revolutionary, the son temporarily seduced
by the silk/wool blend suits and the electric pencil-sharpeners
of the West, and the elder son priggishly rebuked for not
realizing that he had given according to his ability, and ought
to be pleased at a new convert for the Party.

In a thriller, the son would mysteriously disappear with half
the contents of the family safe, suspicion would fall on him
for a number of peculiar incidents, but he would turn up

finally to reveal that the elder brother had been in league with an international Communist drug-smuggling ring. . . .

In a Graham Greene novel, the son would be eaten away with guilt as with worms within; I suspect he would probably never return, except in imagination, but carry his father's agony within him, a personification of the Church's authority, bleeding and crying but not to be mocked; even the harlots would be hell.

Much the same, with a false nose on, from Evelyn Waugh: after a truly disastrous spell among the swine in Djibouti, the dilettante, his friends dead, would return to the ever dottier and more decaying family home, complete with Oxford Movement chapel, a tutor shuffling about in carpet slippers, a father drinking port on a terrace from which the common people might just be glimpsed on a clear day.

A Braine drain, where the young executive makes good, hates it, retraces steps to gritty Plodston in the North. In a children's book, the prodigal would be a locomotive that didn't know how to keep on the rails; it would blow a gasket and, forgiven by the station master, return to the engine shed in which the elder brother was furiously puffing.

A Somerset Maugham play – come to think of it, he's already done it – in which the wretched bad boy marries a millionairess and re-buys the family mansion, elder brother and all; or one by Tennessee Williams, red-eyed, over-heated, in which Big Daddy has always had a not-too-nice yen for the younger, prettier boy; or a dense psychological novel in which the boy has to work out his sexual salvation in brothels and bedsits before rejoining the family breeding ground; here I think the elder brother would be imprisoned by his own inhibitions, the father a shadowy tyrant. We notice there is no mother in the story. *Why not?*

The elder brother should be the really interesting figure, of course – and anyone at day school who has a brother at boarding school readily identifies with him: his case was surely that nothing ever *happens* at home. Why was he so brutally treated, one wonders? He must have coped with the old man's moods all the time the boy was gone; perhaps with veiled insults over the bottle that it is his monkish righteousness, his stuffiness, that drove the lad away . . . 'all that I have is thine', indeed: nobody asked him about his half of the fatted calf.

If I had a novelist handy, I would like it written, I think, in terms of eternal renewal: showing that the boy who copies his father gets only a smudged copy of the old man and his ideals; that the elder brother is unimpressive because his acceptance is too static. The point would be that 'Beauty dies of beauty, worth of worth And ancient lineaments are blotted out'; that only by going away, and trying other things (many of them not entirely unpleasant at the time) can one see the point of anything or bring it fresh reality.

Like Chesterton, who was asked as he packed in Battersea where he was journeying: 'I replied, with a strap between my teeth, that I was going to Battersea.' Why, even the elder brother was only noticed when he absented himself from the feast: the father never even said he was doing a grand job until then. I would get the scribe to write that ere the journey homeward lies, far, far must it remove; and that the longest way round may be the only way you can put up with home once you end up back there.

One may even end up approving of all those ghastly scripture classes at school – or how would any of you have known what on earth I've been talking about?

24 · There's no Accounting for it

Every time I try to keep accounts the same thing happens. I keep meticulous record of every penny, mark the halfpennies *up* to allow for marginal error, check it and copy it into a book; and it all balances exactly except for one pound eighteen and sevenpence. Somehow the hidden sixpences come and go under their own steam, money is not what you make but what you have over at the end of the week, and the whole thing is as mysterious as a splinter sect. But it is nothing to the entirely parallel process of trying to keep account of time.

What *did* happen to Saturday? We started out with sixteen hours in hand; we spent an hour at the shops, an hour cleaning up, say two hours making and eating food; a walk, three-quarters, TV an hour – and now it's midnight. Just as one never reckons up enough hairpins, lollipops, bus fares and sixpences in hats of toothless musicians, so the day goes without any record of the number of times you go into a room and forget what you came for, or try five times for a telephone number, or the seven minutes that invariably elapse between being absolutely ready on one side of the front door and actually out with it shut behind you. You don't notice the minutes that slide past while you tap your teeth or try to think what to do next. Unforgiving minute, indeed; the minute isn't standing there being unforgiving, it's wandered off whistling vaguely through its teeth.

To say that one spends time only actually doing things is like saying you spend only fivers and one pound notes. The unreality of the sort of detective story in which the body is always 'very dead' on discovery and 'not a pretty sight' when revealed is shown, among other things, by their total neglect of this fact. You know their timetables:

12.25	Sir Gerald enters library; pours sherry.
12.30	Maid leaves dining-room, passing open door and seeing him at window.
12.32	Sir Gerald leaves by French windows, crosses garden;
12.34	reaches summer house;
12.38	stabs Marilla La Touche;
12.39–45	lurks behind summer house till gardener passes on way home to dinner;
12.52	conceals body in shrubbery;
12.55	regains library.
1 o'clock	Maid announces that luncheon is served.

Unless the wretch has an alibi for all of that time, he's sunk. But what really happened, of course, was:

12.25	Sir Gerald goes to library;
12.30	decides to have sherry;
12.34	finally finds glass;
12.37	pours sherry;
12.38–59	drinks sherry while gazing absently at small ads upside down on back of *Country Life*;
1 o'clock	lunch at last, thank God.

No one means to act like this, in real life, any more than you plan to have a hole in your purse; but it comes to the same thing in the end.

It's the spaces between the things you do that makes the difference between being frantic or relaxed, humming or dull; it's what makes one woman do so much that everyone else is flat against the walls cushioning the shock, and another believe that making two meals a day for an undemanding man leaves her no time for one part-time hour a week. It's the

99

difference between the office man, whose gaps are his train, his tea-break and snoring in the boardroom, and the home-bound freelance who does eight times as much work one day, and nothing at all on the day he has an appointment in town.

The chewing-gum nature of time is the only thing that might give some sense to the phrase about the leisured Victorian age: if you didn't happen to be working sixteen hours down the mines, getting up at seven for family prayers or running beside a carriage all the way from the station in the hope of a tip for carrying the luggage into the house, you were probably occupied with long, slow tasks that left your mind alone, like butter-churning or walking two miles to see a friend.

Remove the doodling and the dawdling, contract the spaces till you are working under real pressure and it's then, to my mind, that you really get results. The trouble is that only rare spirits can put on the pressure themselves; and there's always such a fight about pressure from outside. It's an educational presumption, for example, that there is something good in itself about the absence of push: exams are wicked because they put the heat on, students' individuality would expand even more (strewth!) without the pressure of competition; if only everyone could be relaxed and take their time everything would be fine. I don't believe it. Whatever therapy or younger children may demand, adults and near-adults need the steam heat; those who don't are just as often flaccid and unimpressive as dazzlingly relaxed.

Maybe I feel this because mine's a trade where no one does any work at all except under pressure (witness all those stock-pile articles that *never* get written during a printing strike). But it's not the only one: I'm told that if you set a man a business problem with all the time in the world, he starts on it half-heartedly, abandons it for something more pressing, and when he finally realizes it's been with him too long, turns in a botched-up version of idea one. Give him a deadline and he will crack down and produce it all in one coherent furnace-forged piece.

Pressure to stay alive, to get the tiger before he gets you, or set your name in the stars is what boosts the human race upwards; and Hemingway's virtue of 'grace under pressure' (and don't say 'Who's she?') seems to me the perennial condition of humanity.

Only you can't keep it up. The boiler will burst, the pressure cooker will run dry; sooner or later only a hollow rattle will result when you shake the golden goose. Things need time to grow back, to fill up, to sort themselves out. This is what dreams do – apparently if you miss a lot of sleep it's the absence of your dreams as much as of your rest that makes you so edgy – and daydreams and picking the teeth do it too.

What you have to have is a *change* of pace, all-out effort at one moment, placid bumbling the next. Simenon writes a book in sixteen days – but not every sixteen days; they had to lock up Mozart in an upper room to get one of his operas finished – thrown page by page out of the window – but he'd hardly have done much if he'd never got out of the attic.

This, at least, can be our excuse for the unaccounted hours; and to the Lizzies who never stop one can always say, as the man said to the Method actor, 'Don't just *do* something – *stand* there.'

25 · A Welcome for Winter

Oh well, there it goes, that thing that was alleged to be summer; and good riddance to it, if you ask me.

The trouble with summer is that you are never let off the inconveniences, no matter how unlike a summer it may have been: you still have to wash the windows because the dirt shows, there still seems to be an unending series of blouses to iron; and even if it snowed all August you would never be let off the lettuce. Indeed, my theory is that when Persephone went down to hell her mother did in fact arrive before she'd eaten the fatal seeds, but the conversation went like this:

Demeter: Come back with me, my darling, and it will be eternal summer on the earth.

Persephone: Does that mean I'll have to wash lettuce all the year round?

Demeter: Well, yes.

Persephone: In that case I'll have a pomegranate.

No doubt for beavers, swallows and people who believe in spring-cleaning April is the beginning of the year; but there must be plenty of us who feel that life really starts up in the autumn. Maybe it's a hangover from the school year; maybe it's because we've spent the summer holidays planning how we will do the winter; maybe it's because we are released from the feeling that we've got to enjoy ourselves because it's summer, see.

But the fall into winter certainly has its points. In winter you can get going on long projects without everybody concerned going on holiday in the middle; there is no incentive to let the children stay up late so you get a bit of evening to

yourself (this is what is meant by the long winter evenings);
and one is highly likely to be afflicted with the sort of wild
optimistic energy that makes people sign up for things they
can't possibly want to learn, like Serbo-Croat and progressive
metallurgy.

This winter, I tell myself, I'll really get it right. I shall go to
bed on the first day of my colds, buy gumboots now and not
later; we will do the Christmas cards in November and write
all the thank-you letters well before Christmas. This year
there will always be soup – the ham-bone one, the pot-au-feu,
the leek soup that wraps you round like an internal blanket;
this year I might even learn the family special, a great con-
coction made by boiling up a stick of celery, a couple of
carrots, a handful of compost and Nanny's garters: 'How did
this tea-leaf get into the soup?' my brother once asked. 'It must',
my father explained, 'have fallen on the floor.' This year we'll
preserve a goose in its own fat, get a wreath for the front door
at Christmas, make snowflakes out of tissue paper, watch TV
programmes and not just television and remember to water
the bulbs. No, really.

It has to be admitted that we are also in for brussels sprouts,
damp mackintoshes and other people's colds. There will be
a great freeze which will take no one by surprise but those
concerned with the supply of gas, coal and electricity; who
will then accuse us of being moral weaklings if we use any
gas, coal or electricity.

Many will buy pretty boots to keep out the wet, and when
the wet comes streaming in will be told: 'But, Madam, these
are *fashion* boots!' There is bound to be at least one fog which
stops you getting to something you want to go to, though
with any luck it should get you out of at least two things
you're trying to avoid; and there will be an acute shortage of
smokeless fuel among those who are forbidden by law to use
anything else. So those in smokeless zones will resort to their

usual trick: as Victorian husbands smoked up the chimney pretending it was coal, so we will pretend that all those blazing logs are just my husband's pipe, officer.

And there is, admittedly, New Year to be got through. First the outbreak that comes with everybody doing TV Show of the Year, Book of the Year, Prize-winning Carrot (Second Class) of the Year (I have often thought, and with Christmas, too, that any paper that had the guts to ignore it altogether would double its circulation).

And there will be New Year's Eve, that cruel festival where everyone wants to be asked out, not to ask; where no one feels the slightest obligation to include the old and lonely, as they do at Christmas; and where you are usually too overstuffed with Christmas to enjoy yourself anyway. We are idiots to have our national jolly in the middle of winter; if you have something like Bastille Day or the Fourth of July everyone can flow out into the open and make merry whether they've any friends or not. Perhaps we could rename it Blitz Day, and celebrate it with blankets and cocoa in the Tube?

One reason we like winter is because it has such strong links with things from long ago: the smell of oil stoves, of being warm in the country; the feel of scented velvet that meant Mother (will my children, I wonder, feel an equal nostalgia for a mixture of Arpège and plastic?), the pleasure of cracking puddle after puddle with the heel of your boot, of skating on a frosty morning or coming home in the early dark to tea and crumpets by the fire. There was bread-and-milk at bedtime, the rustle of the filled stocking in the dark of Christmas morning; the red round sun of a November afternoon with the distant roar of someone else being keen on rugger.

But better even than the extraordinary emptiness of the hard blue air on a wintry morning, with the last beech leaves brown against it; better than crunching tufts of frosted grass under your foot or making the first mark on a field of snow;

better than anything that happens out of doors is the feeling of being *dug in*.

In Mary Norton's *The Borrowers Afield* the finger-sized creatures spend their chilly nights in a ball of fluff, of sheeps-wool; and that is the essence of it. The weather may be (slightly) cooler than summer but you are far warmer; even other people light their fires, you can have a bath, shoot into the hot, smelly mouth of the Underground or pull the sheep-skin round your ears, warmed by the very contrast of your freezing breath streaming out in front of you. The best of winter is to sit in a warm jersey by the fire, drinking mulled wine and reading about all those poor chaps without boots in the freezing mud of the Crimea.

26 · Jane's Economy Kick

Styles of economy are as variable as hairstyles. In Nancy Mitford's Radlett household, you could tell an economy drive by the fact that the writing paper got thinner and the lavatory paper thicker. In *Middlemarch*, poor Lydgate thought the way to save was to buy the best of everything. Some save icecubes; others renew elastic. One man, in debt to the tune of thousands, resolved to give up taking in the *Illustrated London News*, and another gave up smoking in taxis. This is the sad tale of Jane Jones, who had a way of economizing that was all her own.

Her decision to retrench was not greeted with unmixed enthusiasm by her family. They remembered, as she conveniently didn't, the money spent on a journalism course which was to make all their fortunes, and resulted in two unpaid poems in the parish magazine; they recalled the tin-can stove which was going to cut gas bills by boiling kettles on old newspaper. Fortunately it didn't work, or they'd have had to take forty copies of *The Times* a day. Above all they recalled the 'Grow Mushrooms for Profit' kick, which had filled the cellar with smelly straw for a season, and produced one single mushroom only when they'd finally thrown the lot on the rubbish dump. This time, however, she swore there were to be no projects; just sensible rationalization: 'So that it doesn't all go on Crispy Cod Fries, darling,' she explained, 'so that we can have some over and buy antiques or things.'

Like most families that are not totally tee, the drink bill seemed the obvious place to start (no national survey on drinking habits ever brings the confessions up anywhere near the level of the nation's actual consumption). The trouble, Jane decided, was their resolute, hoggish, northern attitude; what was wanted was a casual Mediterranean approach, a glass of wine out of a running bottle; do something for the bags under the eyes as well. She laid out on sound blended wines like Nicolas and Waitrose in litre bottles and bought a few Tritons, those patent bottle-stoppers at 5s 6d each, to seal them up again. It was just bad luck that everyone looked on the litres as a challenge and got through a third as much again in an evening.

But there, said her husband (a telly don of some standing), *everything* to do with money *always* led to drinking more: either you were drinking up the château-bottled rather than laying out for Portuguese rosé, or you were laying in new large quantities of something supposed to be cheap; or you were simply drowning the thought of your overdraft in gin.

Food, too, seemed ripe for economy; too much pre-cooked-pre-packed stuff came into the house anyway. This resulted in a good deal of buying cauliflowers at two bob instead of frozen peas at 1s 4d; a resolution to make a good old apple pie set her back half a crown for the apples instead of 1s 9d worth of expensive foreign guavas; but when it came to cakes she was determined. Not having any cake tins, she bought two (5s 3d each) and set to work; however, she soon found that she was not exactly a demon baker and got on better with a mix; she preferred the American ones at 4s 6d a packet.

Reading in her consumer magazines where it said, she re-solved to buy her household dry goods in bulk from the sort of places that supply prisons, hospitals and Great Hostesses; the saving, bar for bar of soap and roll for roll, was con-siderable. Unfortunately she didn't have the storage space of the Royal Northern or a Royal Duchess, had to consign the stuff to a damp cellar, and kept it in condition only by wrap-

ping it up in the sort of polythene bags you store fur in – at
2s 9d a bag. She had also, without knowing it, ruled out about
the only unconscious economy the household had: a tendency to use old envelopes and pumice stone for days when
the proper supplies had run out. But the family now much
appreciated the large supplies always to hand.

Turning down the heating they liked less, and tended to
get their own back by lighting the oven, huddling over the
clothes dryer and keeping the only electric fire on all day as
the quarterly bills showed only too plainly. But at least her
other failures affected only herself. The attempt to stop buying paperbacks resulted in a cool 16s of library fines. And the
resolve to stop wasting money on taxis meant that the first
time she saved four bobs' worth of taxis by putting 2s in the
meter she collected a ten-bob parking fine; and the second
time went by tube, sat next to a hard-luck lady heading home
to the north, and had been touched for a fiver before they even
reached King's Cross.

Up to this point the Professor, as he was laughingly called
by the TV producers, had watched it all with amused de-
tachment, only continuing to perfect his Time/Money theory
of women. This held that if you had a wife who was very
idle she'd have too much time to spend your money round
the shops; if she was exceedingly busy (like she was earning a
lot herself) she would be liable to spend too much saving
time – telegrams, taxis, express cleaners. Somewhere between
the two was the perfect moment, when she should be too
busy to spend anything; he had got this up as a graph and the
perfection of its curves was his constant study. But now he
saw the grim spectre of the sales looming up on the horizon,
realized that if Jane were allowed loose to save money in them
they could really end up bankrupt, and took everybody off
to a remote farmhouse for a month, where all they could
spend money on was Rentokil and candles. Jane, however,

spent most of the time dreaming of a sunny summer holiday, and when they got back immediately fixed up one in Malta – cheap, but without the Natural Brake of the travel allowance that was then in force.

Further incidents followed. Jane had a notion about spending a lot on Good Quality tights that would wear; except that nothing wears against broken nails and splinters, which were what always did for hers. There was a washing-machine that was bought to cut down the laundry bills; except that they couldn't dry the sheets at home and the Prof couldn't bear the way his shirts were ironed.

'Look, old boy,' a common-room colleague finally said in sympathy, 'The only way to save money is not to *have* any. That's all that keeps any woman in check. Your trouble is that being freelance you pay your tax retrospectively, so there's always too much cash in the bank. Get an accountant, get him to sort out what you owe, get it put out of the way and all this will stop.' So the Prof took his advice, got an accountant, got all the spare cash siphoned off into an untouchable account guarded by two eunuchs and a cobra, and left the current account with nothing more than was needed for absolute necessities like bus fares and his own cigarettes. Later that month the accountant's bill came in. . . .

Only the more preposterous parts of this tale are true. But can any reader tell me who it was who said that any reform whose effect is not the exact opposite of that intended must be accounted a success?

27 · *Cases in Search of A.P.H.*

For some days Mr Joseph Antonelli, owner of the Clink-a-Moo Milk Cart chain of ice-cream vans, had parked his truck outside St Mark's Primary School every morning, to sell children ice-cream on their way *into* school.

This he did with impunity because the Trunk Roads (Prohibition of Way) (Clearways) order of 1963 states that a vehicle cannot so park on a verge or lay-by adjacent to the main road and sell things 'unless the goods are immediately delivered or taken into premises adjacent to the vehicle from which the sale is effected' – which they were, as the children disappeared promptly into the school. The police were finally able to prosecute Mr Antonelli, however, when Mr Gardner, a master at the school, caused one of the children to remain on the roadside for twenty minutes by the production of successive sixpences for further ice-creams. Mr Antonelli was thus liable, and was found Guilty.

*

Mr Justice Mainpipe is no longer, it seems, planning to sue the Government under the Judges Remuneration Act of 1965 because the wine served on his favourite circuit has been changed. The Act says the Government can revise or vary the Judges' remuneration, 'but not so as to reduce the amount of salary previously payable'. Mr Mainpipe maintained that the substitution of 1955 Lynch Bages for the 1948 Château Latour he had previously been served did in fact amount to a drop in salary. His relations, however, have insisted that he retire from the Bench on grounds of what is laughingly called ill-health.

*

Alderman C. Dutty persuaded Eastbourne Borough Council to prosecute three girls whose behaviour he thought immodest for the excessive pollution of the Eastbourne waters by their suntan oils. The Judge pointed out, however, that although the Board of Trade *could* include other descriptions of oil to be subject to the Act 'having regard to the persistent nature of the oil described' it *hadn't* so far said anything about Ambre Solaire, Sun Nivea or the discharge of such from collapsible rubber dinghies; and the case was dismissed.

*

A current libel action is interesting more for personal than for legal reasons. The plaintiff, Jeoffrey Laynewright (known to thousands as the embroidery correspondent of *My Little Home* magazine) is suing his erstwhile friend and flatmate, Garry Andrews, for a libel allegedly contained in the latter's column in the *Evening Gazette*. The article described the cruelty of an old woman who kept her grandchild shut up in a dark flat all day, rarely if ever allowing the child to roll about in the fresh green grass of the park.

According to Mr Laynewright, all this was a thinly concealed attack on his own treatment of his pet chihuahua, which was the subject of the quarrel which ended the flatsharing between the two men. He is bringing in evidence the fact that a milkman shouted 'Ow's the baby?' up at the windows of the flat on the day after the article appeared. Mr Andrews says that he is amazed that anyone could possibly identify a man and his dog with an old woman and a child, and says that the milkman's remark much more probably referred to the play *Spitting Image* (reviewed on the same day as Mr Andrews's article appeared) in which a pair of homosexuals succeed in giving birth to a child. The case continues.

*

One case which never got further than the solicitor was attempted by Mr Joseph Sluggs, labourer. He tried to commit suicide in the top floor of the antiquated building in which he lived by turning on all the gas taps in his flat. On the next floor another tenant tried to fry some sausages and injudiciously struck a match. In the resulting explosion everyone was killed except the would-be suicide, Mr Sluggs, who then attempted to get the Gas Board to pay for the funeral of his wife.

He was apparently inspired by a total misunderstanding of the word 'undertaker' in a section of the Act relating to financial liability between the Gas Board and the undertaker.

*

Then there is a case shortly to be brought under the new Trade Descriptions Act which should command some attention. This Act makes traders liable even for verbal misrepresentations about the 'fitness for purpose' of the goods they sell: if a salesman says a child's wigwam is suitable for camping in the mountains, the shop is liable when the shopper is drenched, even though nothing was written down.

When the Act comes into force, Miss Dolly Sackton is to sue Messrs Barrages about a carpet they sold her, describing it as 'suitable for bedroom use' (the phrase normally used to describe carpet that is not tough enough for stairs or living-rooms). After only eighteen months the carpet is showing shocking signs of wear; Messrs Barrages maintain, however, that Miss Sackton (who describes herself as a model) puts her carpet to excessive wear. Miss Sackton is convinced that if they win she can then sue them again under the Slander of Women Act of 1891 for impugning her good name.

*

An interesting action was brought against Mr Rehaboam Jones, grocer, who contravened the Wild Birds (Sunday in

Anglesey) Order, 1963. This includes Anglesey among the places where birds may be taken and killed on any day of the year outside the close season except on Sundays.

Mr Jones argued that the shooting took place before 1 a.m. on the morning of Sunday 14 July last, so that by nature's (not British Summer) time it was still Saturday. Mr Jones (a freethinker) changed his plea to Guilty when it was explained that the purpose of the Order was not, as he had supposed, to ensure that birds were undisturbed at their devotions. The case was dismissed.

(Apologies to A. P. Herbert)

28 · Battle Cries

Now that people are becoming so much less inhibited about having their rows in public it is essential, if innocent by-standers are to get any fun out of it at all, that we should understand the real implications of the phrases used. Here is a glossary of some battle cries and their meanings:

I had it first! . . . It is the other boy's toy.

It's mine! . . . He had it first.

You may be right . . . I'm tired of the argument.

You never told me that! . . . I wasn't listening when you told me that.

But I told you! . . . Of course I told you – I hope.

Why do you have to be so critical all the time? . . . I have no idea why there are three buttons off your pyjamas.

Why do you have to be so emotional all the time? . . . Stone walling is my most maddening tactic.

Were you really serious yesterday when you said . . . I have just now thought up a crushing reply and want a chance to use it.

You don't love me any more . . . I assume you do love me or I wouldn't risk this remark.

(From dustmen) *We've come to wish you a* MERRY CHRISTMAS . . . Give us five bob or we'll spill your mess over the path for a year.

Of course you know much more about it than I do, but . . . I am about to catch you out in a howling error.

DON'T SHOUT . . . Don't shout back.

(Woman to hairdresser) *Yes, it's fine – just fine – only not quite what I expected* . . . It's perfectly awful but I haven't the nerve to say so.

Darling, you will do it before the weekend, won't you? . . . The job can wait a day or two, but I'm feeling bad-tempered NOW.

I only said it didn't taste the way it usually does/I only asked what had happened to your face . . . My tone of voice was just what I hoped it would be.

God, I've had a frightful day . . . One false move and it will be Your Fault.

It isn't the money that matters . . . It isn't me that's going to pay.

Darling, would you think – I mean, maybe it would be better – I thought – maybe if I drove? . . . You're sloshed.

Look what you've made me do! . . . Why keep a wife and blame yourself?

(From a five-year-old) *Bloody idiot!* . . . I am too small to hit you.

I don't know why there's never any soda water/discipline/matches in this house . . . I don't know why you never provide any.

I've said I'm sorry, haven't I? . . . I'm not sorry, and I'm de-lighted you are giving me an excuse to go on being angry.

All you women/engineers/mothers/Smiths/Welshmen are the same . . . I have run out of arguments.

I won't ask you to my birthday party! . . . The ultimate sanction.

My father's a policeman! . . . Your father is bigger than mine.

Anyway you stink . . . My father is not bigger than your father, my father is not a policeman, you won't ask me to your birthday party.

Why do you always? . . . It's war.

(From Judge to Barrister) *I hear what you say* . . . But can hardly believe my ears.

You know her far better than I do, of course . . . Only too well, by the sound of it.

I suppose it would be too much to ask . . . If I asked in the ordinary way, you might say yes, and then where's my grievance?

Look, why don't you get some sleep/ We're not getting anywhere like this/ We'd better talk this over calmly some other time . . . I can best enrage you by implying that you are hysterical.

I wouldn't mind if only he'd let me know he wasn't coming – it's such bad manners/ I wouldn't mind if only he'd be open about it/ I wouldn't mind if she was someone you could respect . . . I would mind anyway; the detail gives me something I can decently complain about.

I don't know how you could even think of such a thing . . . You've already dropped the project, but I haven't finished yet.

Have you quite finished? . . . I am ignoring everything you've just said.

Mummy's very tired, dear . . . Mummy will understand that I mean she's lost her temper.

Daddy's been too busy to mend it, dear . . . Daddy will understand that I think he's loafed all week.

Do we have to watch television – couldn't we read?/ Do we have to read – couldn't we just talk? . . . Why aren't you making love to me?

Joe's wife doesn't mind if he gets in late . . . I've not discussed the matter with Mrs Joe.

I don't want to open it all up again, but . . . I want to fire one last shot – and if you reply, the rest of the row's on you.

Why do you have to justify yourself all the time? . . . Don't think you can get out of it just by being in the right.

29 · *Fine and Private Place*

I am in my bath. I do not wish to be disturbed. I don't care if the house is burning down, the Government falling, the pound in ruins and all the hogs escaping. No doubt the children will stop crying eventually, someone else will turn off the beans; the National Debt you just have to learn to live with and worse things happen at sea. Anyway, I'm in my *bath*.

I know a man with a gazebo to retire to; there are doubtless some lighthouse keepers who get a bit of time to themselves; the religious go on retreats and people sometimes get a little enviable privacy, stuck in a lift between two floors. But for the rest of us, the bath is the only refuge. Nobody can get at us, nobody can expect us to get up and make their tea or sort their knitting or answer the telephone. Andy Capp crashed the last sacred barrier when, Florrie being in her bath and the doorbell ringing, he said, 'You go, pet – I've got me boots off.' And those carefully nudist parents who believe in 'open bathroom' as a psychological aid can go take a running shower at themselves; there has to be some way of getting away from the little voice saying, 'You *have* got a fat tummy.'

It's no wonder that it is now the bathroom that the decorators attack with their greatest zest. Sunk baths and baths in the middle of a room, a shower out of a metal chandelier; a round white bath with a gold key pattern round the edge or a bath with four-poster curtains are all perfectly available possibilities, and flowered basins, crystal jars, lush dripping vines and gilt taps and silk chairs and carpets are becoming commonplace. These days you don't even need to take anything into the bathroom with you to think: you just lie there planning the dream bathroom in which you would like to be floating.

Usually it's the exact opposite of the one you're in, of course. The family bathroom is always entirely filled with steam, so that when you *do* find your underclothes they're damp; the pundits say to run the two taps together, but how can you tell how much hot water there'll *be*? The lock on the door rarely works, and anyway what you really want is a lock in the other sense – a people-lock like an air-lock, so that you can't even hear them beating on the door. And although most bathrooms look all right from above, architects almost never seem to lie down in the bath half-way through their labours: the fish-eye view is too often of the pipes under the basin, the unpainted bottom of the medicine cabinet, the crack that you keep meaning to do something about on the ceiling. (Le roi soleil spent 24,000 livres on gilding his bathroom ceiling. Now there was a man who knew what he was about.)

We can reject with horror, of course, the whole idea of the *cold* bath. The ancient Greeks had this dread habit of belting up and down the side of their cold baths in a spirit of aspiration and Dr Arnold (not to say a temperature of ninety in the shade); the Romans, though still imbued with far too much of the empire-building spirit, at least had the sense to heat the thing up; but it was left to the blessed Turks to give up the PT altogether and just lie there waiting to be scraped, like so many lumps of fat being rendered down for cooking.

The shower, too, strikes me as an irrelevance. The trouble is not only that the three things you cannot do in a shower, as Ogden Nash said, are read and smoke and get wet all over; you can't paint your nails or have a cup of coffee or watch television or eat chocolates or come to great and earth-shaking decisions (like whether to turn the hot tap on again). In a bath, you can do all these things just about simultaneously;

and no doubt the Australians, now absurdly addicted to showers, will come round to proper baths in time just as the Americans, that other emergent nation, now seem to be doing.

Swimming in shoals is also a lot of red herrings, if you ask me. Japs bathe communally, the Finnish sauna should be a social event and indeed, to the really addicted, a solitary sauna is about as much fun as a solitary cocktail party. But the emotions of the beach party and those of the proper womb-like amniotic bath are totally different: only twins, one imagines, could enjoy a bath together – whatever others may be enjoying it isn't the bath. For the whole point of a bathroom is that it is yourself.

What is the difference, after all, between a really delightful drawing-room, or bedroom for the matter of that, also very personal, also very pleasant, and this terrific draw of the bathroom? It is that it is entirely selfish. It's impossible to imagine anyone leaping out of a hot bath and going out to reform the world. I know a woman who said her prayers in the bathroom, but I bet it was harder than anywhere else in the house. And when I dictate letters in the bath (dictaphone, you ass) it's a constant struggle not to make them even more supercilious or maudlin than usual.

This is where I think the decorators may be getting carried away in the wrong direction. You don't want to bring too much of the world into the bathroom or it is no longer part of you. The illusion is that the walls of the bathroom are your walls, that the iridescent curtains, the gold bottles and the rich green scent are your walls, your scent: a shell in which one's own pink shrinking insignificant self is glorified, the face cream and its gilded jar equally a part of the illusion. What one is after is a bigger, prettier, glossier exterior – not one with a whole lot of other hermits getting in on the crab-shell, too.

For the same reason, it should be small and enclosed: Rita Hayworth singing 'Bewitched, Bothered and Bewildered' in *Pal Joey* behind all those amber screens, and the actress who said she had so many mirrors in her bathroom she could see herself in seventeen different places (to which Beverley Nichols remarked that he didn't know women *had* so many places) are both trying to extend the thing too much into the open: it is the enclosed grotto which is perfection.

Status used to be clothes, then it was kitchens; now that it's bathrooms I suspect we're back to clothes again. This year I shall be wearing pink foam, green glass and a couple of new pictures; and I don't care how hard you laugh because I can't hear you at all.

30 · When They Grow Up

When you are small, you have a grand category of ambition: when I'm grown up. When I'm grown up, you say, I'll go up in Space. I'm going to be a Nauthor. I'll kill them all and *then* they'll be sorry. I'll be married in a cathedral with sixteen bridesmaids in pink lace. I'll have a puppy of my *own* and no one will be able to take him away. As Eartha Kitt said in some play, when I'm grown up I'll be a rich white woman; or as Jean Webster put it, I'll marry an undertaker and be an inspiration to him in his work.

None of it ever happens, of course – or darn little; but the fantasies give you the idea that there is something to grow up for. Indeed one of the saddest things about gilded teenage is the feeling that from eighteen on, it's all downhill; I read with horror of an American hippie wedding where someone said to the groom (age twenty) 'You seem so kinda grown up somehow', and the lad had to go round seeking reassurance that he wasn't, no *really* he wasn't. A determination to be better adults than the present incumbents is fine, but to refuse to grow up at all is just Peter Pan in a Viva Zapata moustache.

Right, so then you get some of what you want, or something like it, or something that will do all right; and for years you are too busy to do more than live in the present and put one foot in front of the other; your goals stretching little beyond the day when the boss has a stroke or the moment when the children can bring you tea in bed – and the later moment when they can actually bring you *hot* tea, not mostly slopped in the saucer. However, I have now discovered an even sweeter category of ambition. When my children are grown up. . . .

When my children are grown up I'll learn to fly an aeroplane. Undeterred even by the thought of Aunt Ada Doom in her Amy Johnson kit, I will career around the sky, knowing that if I do go pop there will be no little ones to suffer shock and maladjustment; that even if the worst does come to the worst I will at least dodge the geriatric ward and all that looking for your glasses in order to see where you've left your teeth. Or I could be a barmaid, at last; too late then, I suppose, to develop blonde hair and a big bosom and lean lusciously across the beer slops, but I could go in for iron-grey waves and a cosy apron, and if they did call me Mum at least they wouldn't make it a two-syllable word on a falling inflexion the way the little beasts do now.

All sorts of gleeful things spring to mind. I could write some terribly sincere memoirs with names and hope that, like Galahad Threepwood, I would be paid thousands to suppress them. I could start breakfasting upstairs again on cheese and a Thermos of coffee. Some days I feel I would even have the strength to sail into the *Observer* and reorganize all; the fact that no one would be fool enough to let me is neither here nor there. When my children are grown up I'll have fragile, lovely things on low tables; I'll have a white carpet; I'll go to the pictures in the afternoon. When the children are grown up I'll actually be able to do a day's work in a day, instead of spread over three, and go away for a weekend without planning as for D-day. When I'm grown up – I mean when they're grown up – I'll be *free*.

Of course, I know it's got to get worse before it gets better. Twelve-year-olds, I'm told, don't go to bed at seven, so you don't even get your evenings; once they're past ten you have to start worrying about their friends instead of simply shooing the intruders off the doorstep, and to settle down to a steady ten years of criticism of everything you've ever thought or done or worn. Boys, it seems, may be less of a trial than girls, since they can't get pregnant and they don't borrow your clothes – if they *do* borrow your clothes, of course, you've got even more to worry about; but no description makes these years sound like anything but an Arthur Bryant: The Tortured Years would be about right.

The young don't respect their parents any more, that's what. Goodness, how sad. Still, like eating mussels, it might be all right once you've got over the idea: it might let *us* off having to bother quite so much with them when the time comes. The younger generations don't seem any less likely than their predecessors to pay our hospital bills or bail us out of jail; they're quite good-hearted; but any parent who doesn't know in advance that she will be allowed no share in her children's emotions is ostriching in the sands of time. And since, with our borrowed kidneys and aluminium hips, we are all going to live longer anyway, I don't see that this could not be reckoned an advantage. One is simply not going to be able to drone away one's days, toothless in an inglenook brooding on the past.

And this is why my notion is possibly not so potty as it sounds. About once a week I get a letter from some lively and intelligent woman who doesn't feel she has the right thing to do; and however rosy a picture you can paint of courses and part-time work available generally, they never seem to be available at all in the area where she actually lives. Sometimes the trouble is that they've started thinking about it all too late – they could perhaps have settled in a different place, or got a grant if they'd applied younger, or used Uncle Edwin's nest-egg a different way. Even people with no aim of any sort can feel a dreadful flatness when, from being vitally necessary to four or five people for twenty years, they find themselves reduced to gloomily frying the fish fingers for just the one old man.

Yet nothing is more grotesque, nothing irks the young more (for what that's worth) than their stumbling elders trying to keep in step with them. I reckon one shouldn't be looking back, and if the family ain't what it used to be, it works both ways. If I have to give up my old pipe dream of being an appalling old lady terrifying my descendants through a lorgnette, at least I can make plans to devote myself to claret or digging or blackmail instead. Why, I might even revive an ambition I had when I was twelve and start a co-operative laundry.

It would be just my luck, of course, if the fashion changed in the next fifteen years and the young suddenly became clinging and deferential. But the odds are against it. Come to think of it, I've never been a bookie, either . . .

31 · Slim Volumes of Verse

Are you, too, trying to get thinner
Renouncing snacks and tea and dinner?
Take heart! Throughout the ages long
Others have sung the same sad song.

'Oh push away the groaning plate
My figure's in a dreadful state.
Oh tip the grinning whisky out
For I am getting far too stout!
Remember she who wastes away
Lives to eat another day.'

At least we know we're not alone.
We sad reducers are at one
With all those nuts who go to seek
Will-power at forty quid a week
At Shrublands or at Enton Hall
We have a bond – we know it all.

And when it comes to sleight of mind
We're kin, too, with a different kind:
The cleric, wreathed in double chins,
Who says that Lent expunges sins
And – by coincidence – renounces
The foods that pile on pounds and ounces.

Nor is it just this century:
Slimmers abound in history;

So let us turn the pages back
And see how they took up the slack.

*   *   *

When Eden's bliss was torn by doubt
And God Almighty threw them out.
The trouble started with an apple.
Poor Adam simply wished to grapple
With spuds, pies, cakes upon his plate
– But Eve was keen on losing weight.
Jehovah's voice then split the skies:
'Get out – and take some exercise!'

And grim PT, be sure of this,
Was prevalent in gloomy Dis
Where Sisyphus, with groans and sighing,
Pushing his stone uphill, was trying
To get a bit of exercise
And beat his waistline back to size.

Bacchantes, too, thought much the same:
They wrecked the place in Bacchus's name
Indulging in a sort of gym
Determined not to look like him.
And in Greece, too, the silver moon
Shone on fat acolytes aswoon:
'We wax and wax and wax again:
Artemis! teach us how to wane!'

Perhaps the husks the swine did eat
Were just the son's new slimming treat?
(And after that – you have to laugh –
They offered him the fatted calf!)

127

And Nebuchadnezzar, King of Jews,
Had weight, not just a throne, to lose
Among his other madman's ways
He ate the grass for days and days.

Then take the Romans on their couches
They ate and ate, the greedy slouches,
Till they were reeling, sick and hot;
Then thankfully threw up the lot

And settled down to eat again.
We view their manners with disdain
But had they not, though crude and reeking,
Found the one answer we're all seeking?
– Around the festal table seated,
The way to lose your cake and eat it?

Indeed, they knew a thing or two
That well could profit me and you:
Take Julius Caesar, come to that,
Who wanted men about him fat –
The motive must have been ulterior
To make the fatties feel inferior.

The Christian saints all, more or less,
Were good at mortifying flesh;
But I can't bring myself to think
That saying No to food and drink
Rates the word 'Saint' before the name
– For you and I do just the same.

'Drink no more water,' said St Paul.
'But take a little wine, that's all.'
He'd found out, too, that come the crunch
A drink's less calories than lunch.

Perhaps those nuns bricked in a wall
With water were not killed at all.
But let out later, thin and pure
The better for their slimming cure?

Rabelais knew there was no cheating:
'The appetite improves with eating'
His characters were gay, defiant –
But every blasted one a giant.

Are you, I wonder, moved to try it
That fallacy, the liquid diet?
Remember Falstaff, when Hal said
'Monstrous! But one ha'porth of bread
To this intolerable deal
Of sack.' Alas, it made a meal:
And e'en Baconians, sly as sin,
Don't yet suggest that Falstaff's thin.

And nor was Lady Hamilton,
Who at the end weighed thirteen stone
'Twas fear of being overlain
That sent her swain to sea again
With *less* of Lady Hamilton
Trafalgar mightn't have been won.

And so we come to Henry King,
Who chewed those little bits of string.
No doubt he wanted to be slim –
But look at what it did to him!
(And if you don't know where to look
Track down the thing in Belloc's book.)
At his last words we shed a tear,
And I can now adapt them here.

'Oh slimmers all, be warned by me
That breakfast (cut out lunch and tea)
Are all that we should be requiring
– Plus Scotch and eggs before retiring.'

32 · King Baby

The Emperor does not, of course, get up to fetch his own food, let alone cook it; any more than he trots off to his tailor for a fitting – his clothes come to him. He does not fuss about their details – minions do that, just as expert decorators do up his rooms; he simply lets out a blast of contumely if he dislikes the result. Like Louis XIV, he receives, if he has a mind to, at stool. He does not wade through long boring papers when he can perfectly well have them read aloud to him. Their digestions and their sex lives are all that Emperors have to attend to themselves, and this Emperor, not being inclined for sex, can give his entire mind to his digestion. Or whatever it is that babies give their minds to. For to be so powerful that you need do nothing, and so helpless that you can do nothing, are just about interchangeable states.

Men like to think themselves Emperors; women often feel they're more like babies. But different cultures take it differently. A Canadian trapper would think any man unbearably soft who couldn't gut and cook his own rabbit; to most Italians this would be strictly kitchen work, fit only for women. If one of Kinsey's American women bestrides her mate, she is described as dominant – but the ancient Romans did all right with the ancient Romanesses on top, it was just a question of getting someone else to do the work.

In one social bracket the man is the fixer because the woman doesn't know how; in another, all the fixing is done by girl secretaries to leave the tycoon free. Which is the position of power?

It is all this cultural uncertainty which is the cause of the trouble. And the trouble I'm talking about is the trouble we women have getting to work on time or mending fuses or digging the flowerbed or getting the car to start.

Quite a lot of us must have been wondering, as we gloomily dug the car out of the snow last week, what had gone wrong with the female revolution; and I have just discovered the answer. It's all a plot: the men have been playing back at us the technique by which *we* must, all those thousands of years ago, have got out of digging the turnips or delivering ewes at four o'clock in the morning. They have realized, as we have forgotten, that you can get people saddled with almost any amount of work so long as you disguise it as any amount of power.

The major ploy in this is the 'God, you're clever' approach. A really subtle man will make no move actually to ask his female to do the thing – mix the drink, captain the trawler, get the moss off the lawn. He will start by doing it himself, rather badly (a major suffragette plank was how much better women could run the world if only . . .). He puts himself in the position of someone fiddling about with a key in a lock, knowing that it's only a matter of time before the other party can't bear it any longer and says, 'Here, let *me* try.' Then he exclaims. He falls back. If he is devious enough, he may even seem disgruntled – witness the smoke screen about the toughness of women in our society – but underneath he knows he's won. He may tell you you're a genius to be able to fix the heater, to hold down a job, or a burglar, but is he, in fact, standing there admiring your efforts? He is not. He is lying on the back of his neck watching the Cup Final.

When this major effort fails, there are other ploys to adopt, such as the 'What, *now*?' approach. In this the man gladly undertakes to do whatever you want; but nothing then happens. You pass from little hints to greater hints to downright insult, and finally to the point at which you seize the

Black and Decker from his lifeless grasp and say, in effect, 'Infirm of Purpose! Give *me* the daggers.' Actually Lady Macbeth was vainly trying to get her mate actually to *finish* a job and tidy up before the household woke (what, *now?*), another near-impossible task, but the principle's the same.

The only counterploy is to match his inactivity with a lassitude equal to his own; it's true that while you are sitting each other out on who ought to have phoned the builder about the roof the house may actually collapse about your heads, but that's modern marriage.

Then there is the 'Just this Once' technique men use – look at all those people who got stuck with jobs For the Duration, ha, ha. You deliver a parcel or order the booze just once – before you know where you are it'll be your fault if the house runs out. Or suppose that Incapability Brown, our modern hero, used to go shopping with you of a Saturday morning (having rested all week at his desk). By prudently standing between you and the light when you are matching cottons and getting wound up in the leads of Alsatians he soon gets himself let off that jaunt, but he still shifts things from the boot of the car when you get back.

Then one day he's just getting dressed to go out when you get back . . . nothing that day happens to be very heavy. . . . 'Could you possibly manage, love? Just this once?' Probably he will cunningly go back to lifting the boxes meekly for a week or so; and then one day, when you are saying in that high controlled tone that precedes the actual screaming, 'Do you *think* you could get the boxes in now, dear?' He comes out with it: 'But you managed fine by yourself the other day.' *Biffed.*

Mind you, this technique doesn't work all on its own; the man must have been working for years to establish the principle that the only jobs he does are the ones which she cannot, physically, perform (the only two jobs I am *never* stuck with are making tax returns and soda water). We let ourselves in for this, I must admit, by using their alleged muscle as an argument why they should carry this or lift that; actually modern man keeps his muscle only just flexible enough to get a whisky off the sideboard ('While you're up, dear . . .'), but they keep *us* in condition with the aid of all those males in industry who make ladies' models of spades and shears and all those miserable lightweight hods.

Margaret Mead says that there is no job which has not been an all-male job in some community, and an all-female job in another; the only difference is that where men do it, it's regarded as high-powered and difficult, and if it's women's work it's a lowly chore. At the rate we're going the only job left to carry high prestige as a male exclusive will soon be the art of doing absolutely nothing at all.

33 · Interviews

Good morning, I'm from the Personalized Approaches Bureau; we feel that you as a housewife ought to have a real say in what is offered to you, and we simply want to find out what *you* think. Now would you look through this folder? Thank you. Which advertisement did you remember particularly?

The Wilkinson Sword, the Guinness one, the – the one for bread I suppose it was, all country—

Margarine, yes. Would you say you remembered them because they were Arresting, Unusual, Lovable, Amusing or Well Presented?

I'd seen them on telly, see.

Ah. Well, now the one on page eight. Would you say it was Arresting, Unusual, Lovable . . . ?

The one with no teeth? Oh no, I didn't like *that*. Road safety, was it?

Toothpaste. Why would you single that one out especially, do you think?

Well, you did ask.

Yes, well, shall we write that one down as Arresting, then?

*　　*　　*

And our next guest is Mr Thelmus Arrowsap, who's just got back from studying the home life of the Canadian Eskimo in the Antarctic. And I think you spent the last six months actually living with them in their – tepees, is it?

Well, the last ten years, actually.

But even in that short time you obviously got to know them very well. So you must now be in a fairly unique position to pronounce on this question of whether there is any truth in those rumours of cannibalism?

Oh, none whatever – in fact—

But it could, wouldn't you say, have been the presence, one might almost say the exploitation, of the American oil companies that drove them to such extremes?

Oil companies?

Still, if we can get away from that aspect and bring matters closer to home, do you really think such esoteric studies at the taxpayer's expense are justified?

But it was the Icefloe Trust that financed the whole thing—

I'm sorry to leave that question unresolved, Mr Arrowsap, but time's running out on us; thank you very much for coming along.

*　　*　　*

You see, we're from *Rag*, the Glastonbury University student newspaper, and to fill up the gaps on the feature pages we're doing the stuff about famous Actresses and I think you've just done a tour of the Middle East?

Spain, actually. That—

Really? Oh, this could be quite interesting, then. We're terribly keen on Spain at Glastonbury – well, not keen exactly, I mean we absolutely hate Franco, of course; Ronnie – that's my, well, you know, he nearly got thrown out of Spain for being rude about the regime but we're very sympathetic to the *idea* of Spain, if you see what I mean.

Er – not quite, but—

Well, just take me for example, I come from an absolutely middle-class background, my father managed this colliery and my mother thought she was rather county, so I never ever *heard* about Spain until Susie, that's my sister, started trying to import these divine Spanish rugs – we thought it was the culture, then, sort of – you see what I mean?

Er – look, can I lend you a pencil?

Oh no. I never have to write anything down. We're very professional on *Rag* – I can remember everything you've told me. Well, thank you so much, it's been absolutely fascinating . . .

*   *   *

Welcome, Mr Porterhouse, and may I ask how you're liking it here?

Fine, just fine; though I may be biased by the fact that my book *Queen Elizabeth and I Slept Here* – it's out tomorrow published by my good friends Dodder and Rowton – is set in this town.

But of course you've been here before – do you notice many changes?

Well, of course the public's so much more conscious of history than they were. When I published *Queen Anne is Dead* it only sold a few thousand copies, that was in 1959; now it's selling in Pandora Paperbacks – only 2s 6d, of course – off every bookstall.

As an American, do you have any views on this latest French-British row that involves America, I believe?

Well, it concerns me very personally, of course, since they are due to start filming *Mary, Queen of Hearts* in Brittany next month and I'm very worried about that. But I imagine the good sense of both countries will prevail: I guess the public's pretty much the same anywhere, they just like to see good movies and read good books. . . .

*   *   *

Now, Smithers, I want you to understand that the Modern Army isn't just standing around on a parade square. It's essentially a very professional business. People have their different work, of course; but cooks or generals, I think we all like to look on it as just a Job to be Done. Do you have any special bent, I wonder?

I think I'd get in all right, sir. I mean like you're lying there in the trench and the bullets is pissing round like hailstones and they're coming at you and your best mate's got 'is 'ead blown off and you're all spattered with his brains and then they're right up close and you *stick* the bayonet . . . I think you could count on me, sir.

Ah. Yes. Well, perhaps a job in the Pay Corps might be the most satisfactory from *every* point of view. . . .

*   *   *

Do sit down, Miss – or shall I just call you Annunciata? How long have you been in England?

Since two months.

But you speak English fluently?

Prego?

Oh, never mind. Do you cook? My husband and I are very fond of Italian food.

In my home, my mozer she cook for all.

I see. Well, of course, the work's mostly with our four children – you have had much to do with children?

I am much with my young brother.

And he is how old?

Eighteen.

Oh. Now about babysitting; we go out a lot in the evenings and you would be alone in the house – you wouldn't mind that?

My class is Tuesday, Wednesday, Friday and Saturday evening.

Yes. Yes, well, is there anything you'd like to ask me?

You want me when?

If you could start Monday – or even sooner, of course, if you'd like to. . . .

34 · Their Blessed Plots

For the ordinary half-hardy gardener, the year is nine months long.

It starts in March, with crocuses, whose function is simply to catch the gardener's attention before the weeds are already in charge. In April we see with surprise and pleasure that some of the bulbs have actually come up – some in flower, others lying on the earth where the squirrel has left them. In May we buy bedding plants, many of which die, and in June we sit back and look at the roses. By August, a month designed by God for coinciding with the school holidays and offering nothing much but seed pods and greenfly, we have written off this year and dream of our plans for next – next August, that is, it being as hard to think of a season you aren't in as to remember one tune while whistling another. In October we may have a fit of passionate destruction, but by November nothing in the world would get us out at all – except, of course, the arrival of all those blasted plants we idiotically ordered in August.

Not so the experts. They have their own year altogether. They have, for example, this ritual April keening about the state of the lawn. In real life people either pay no attention to the lawn at all until you actually can't see whether you've left the tea things out or not; or they fuss at it all the time, hoiking up dandelions, purging the moss, abolishing couch grass. The main difference between the two is that the neglected lawn is always green with plantains, while the cared-for one is generally yellow with weedkiller.

By August they are bothering about next year's tulips, for

heaven's sake; and in the autumn they are in their element, laying all those fuses which will blow us up next spring. As Geoffrey Taylor of the *Guardian* says, what puts one off gardening in the spring is the way the experts say, 'On ground which has been fully prepared in the autumn. . . .' For a short time in November, when actual gardens are dark and sour, the columns bloom with an exotic profusion of little-known lilies, hothouse orchids and miniature trees; but the all-time record in space filling is held by George Seddon who, at the time of some riots in the British Embassy garden in Moscow, wrote a richly factual piece about how to make your garden demonstrator-proof.

There is a moment of relief around Christmas, when they recommend presents ('for gardening in the lounge a plastic watering-can,' said *The Times*), but after that they go clean off their heads. Scrape the bark of your fruit trees, they urge hysterically; or they tell us what to do with the undershelves in the greenhouse. Winter pruning was presumably invented to give them something to write about in January other than gnomes and fencing; even as it is they urge you to do ridiculous things like getting the mower fixed before the others do, and oiling the blades of hoes: anyway, how can you oil them in January? They're all wet. Experts make appalling use of the phrase: 'Now is the time to': the man can't surely mean *now*, while I'm sitting in front of the fire reading his newspaper? Time enough, surely: like my friend who came in for tea one cold March day and said: 'I've done a month's work out there today. Only trouble is, the month was November.'

Their very language is defeating to most of us. There is this use of the passive voice: 'Care must be taken not to allow plants to dry out. . . .' Imagine yelling 'Care must be taken not to walk on the flower-beds' at your children. They make unconscious assumptions about our resources, with talk of potting-up, hardening-off, or taking out a seed drill; even the humane ones suggest moving this or that to a spare bed, which one would no doubt be happy to do if someone didn't happen to be spending the night in the only one there is.

And they make inexorable use of the decent obscurity of a learned language. Roy Hay saying 'People wishing to plant a variegated shrub tend to think of *Elaeginus pungens maculata*' (they do?) is almost enough to make one join Frances Perry's crusade for avoiding the ugly Latin descriptions (like aster and veronica) and sticking only to our lovely native names (like bonytip fleabane and sneezeweed).

The gardening writers have, I'm told, a very depressing postbag, all about what to do with dark, muddy corners in exceptionally cold parts of Yorkshire. For all that, there are the questions we dare not ask. How long, for example, will bedding plants keep in the boot of the car, given a grey week, a drying wind and acid fumes of about pH4? When you have caught the slugs in the orange skins and dropped them in the salt water, what do you then do with the resulting slug-and-saltwater cocktail? (Pulling the plug is no answer – small gritty stones stay in the bowl for weeks.) Will last year's seeds, filed and forgotten, come up if planted or not?

And, above all, how do you tell when anything is dead? If you dig it up and throw it on the compost it will flower there happily; but otherwise? The other day I rushed in on my husband crying, 'Peace is not dead!'; it gave him quite a turn, he thought I was a student. What, indeed, to do about *him*, and the fact that no one does any digging except me and that ruddy squirrel?

The gardening writers are, when all's said and done, up against a hopeless paradox. Half the time we just want things to produce as much colour for as little effort as possible. In this mood, we want paving stones and not grass, shrubs as tolerant as a sailor's wife, bedding plants and no greenhouse;

we go eagerly for plants condemned as 'invasive', buy all-purpose sprays for the insects and absolutely never get the staking done in time.

But the very fact that we're at it at all implies another side: a side in which we positively wallow in trouble. Then those jobs like stopping the chrysanthemums and disbudding sweet peas become fun; we almost welcome an esoteric disease to nurse the plants through and we constantly attempt new things, not just as a triumph of hope over experience, but to have something fresh to fuss over. The gardening writers, I suppose, know this perfectly well; for if it wasn't so, what would we be doing reading them at all?

I forgot what genius it was said that all young married women were worried because they either were, or were not, going to have a baby. All gardeners worry because it is, or is not, raining. And I suppose the gardening writers worry because they have not, *or have*, solved all our problems for the time being. That, we can agree, would never do.

35 · *Now it Can be Told*

Alas, poor Critick! The twenty-two-year-old 'Critics' programme has gone out for the last time. I don't know how upset its half-million listeners were, or whether they all moved peaceably over to 'The Arts', a programme conveniently discovered for fobbing off anyone who was indignant about the end of 'The Critics'; but the people who were on the programme will mourn indeed. Imagine actually being paid to go to a film, theatre, or art gallery, and then sit down to discuss it after a good lunch.

Not that it always ran smoothly. There was a time when Lionel Hale, tired of having a shirt-sleeved arm constantly waving across him towards the chairman, reached out his jaw and bit it. There was the time all the critics walked out, because they had said the first Reith lecture was terrible, and added for good measure that lectures of this sort were a nonsense anyway; and the BBC cut the whole item (though some of them seeped sheepishly back over the years).

Margaret Lane was sometimes to be seen flat on the floor having a migraine, and there was one occasion when a lady critic, helpfully making conversation, said 'Do tell me, I've often wondered, what *is* action painting?' and the art critic said, 'You stupid bitch, if you don't know what action painting is you shouldn't be on this programme,' and *she* walked out. . . .

In the matter of art I suspect a lot of us were not really fit. It was a salutary experience, though, to go into a gallery showing as it might be nine identical paintings of a white dot on a brown ground, and know that you'd better not come out till you'd found something to say about it. You could certainly endear yourself to the listeners by saying it looked like nine white golfballs on nine brown cowpats and who the hell cared, but would you be asked on the programme again if you did? Actually we often talked longest about the art, just because there was so little to say that everyone padded frantically – the best ploy here was to switch to literature. 'It is essentially the same conception as the work of his fellow-countryman Alexis Kivi. . . .'

The beauty of this, of course, was that you not only got yourself off the art hook, you might, with luck, score for knowing about Alexis Kivi. You got about one point for having read something else by the author of the book, two for having seen the play of the film, three for having seen the play in New York, and four for a personal quotation – 'I remember Rouault said to me once . . .'. Highest marks of all came when we were doing a translation, if you had already read it in the original.

There were lots of tricks at a more mundane level, however. You avoided Wimbledon week if you could, because they put on tennis instead of the repeat and you didn't get so much money; late July and August were also to be given a wide berth because too few new things were happening and you were all too apt to find yourself watching a film in flickering Bulgarian in a minute cinema down the Edgware Road. Some critics always wrote everything down in note form, and when the chairman said 'John Smith, do you agree with that?' they would say, 'I both agree and disagree, but surely the whole point is . . .' and read away (chairmen of character sometimes managed to drop something over the notes at this point). Barbara Bray had a great trick of staring down at the table as she spoke so that the chairman couldn't catch her eye and indicate that enough was enough; one or two who shall be nameless would change tack completely if they found too many people were agreeing with them; and no one talked too much at the preliminary discussion if there was a shark around noted for stealing your best crack and using it.

It must have been puzzling to the listener how seldom we did all agree – especially, of course, over humour: I was always, myself, failing to realize that some foreign film was even supposed to be funny and sitting stonily through it all in an empty cinema at five in the afternoon. Our language may have maddened them, too – though for every person who hated the chat about tonal values and spatial concepts and interpretive pastiche there must have been three at least who *liked* being brained by culture in this way.

More off-putting was perhaps the convention that we all addressed each other by our full names: 'No, no, Katharine Whitehorn, I can't agree with that', somehow sounding as remote from spoken English as the *Daily Express* quotations from ordinary housewives: 'My husband, forty-three, a lorry driver, always says . . .'. And the fact that the ums and ers and hiccoughs were eliminated from the tape – 590 cuts in one programme I believe the record was – made it all sound unduly pat: as one chairman put it, 'It flowed over the air like oil.'

Another thing that was a handicap was the lunch itself – or rather the fact that it was then followed by the preliminary discussion (at which we were all very witty) and only towards the siesta hour by the programme itself. Keeping the alcohol level right was one of producer Lorna Moore's hardest jobs. A hard drink before, beer with and a Scotch after the lunch was the rule, until Cyril Ray complained that the whisky sent him to sleep and the beer sent him to the lavatory when it was his turn to speak; he started bringing wine, and the BBC tried to charge him corkage . . . back to beer and spirits. Then film critic Derek Prowse persuaded Carleton Greene himself, no

less, that a chap as sensitive as he, Derek, couldn't be expected
to perform on crude spirits, and wine was actually provided
for a short time; unfortunately it made several of the critics
so sleepy that the producers got tired of cutting out the snores
and cut out the wine instead.

What finally got the programme killed? One has to admit
it was inflexible – though they did take the whole lot to the
Son et Lumière at Greenwich once, to Harlow New Town,
and to Coventry Cathedral (when they had plodded round
that and were heading thankfully for home the art critic suddenly said fiercely: 'But we haven't seen it in action!' and
made them sit through a service). But there had to be equal
weight given to all the subjects, everybody had to have their
say on everything; better far, some thought, to let just two
men fight it out if they'd a mind to, or take up most of the
programme on the most valuable item and dismiss the others
– they do, after all, in magazines; even in newspapers sometimes toy with the idea. Perhaps it was too highly categorized
– it's impossible to imagine the critics trotting off to a happening at the Round House or a mixed rave down the King's Road.

But, in fact, half the things that could be criticized about the
programme were on the mend by the time it was condemned: recording was in the morning before the lunch, the
preliminary bit of scripted prose at the beginning of each
item had been dropped; the discussion generally was much
more of a free-for-all.

I suspect myself that it was the in-group feeling of it all that
made people hostile: this gentlemanly club atmosphere of 'we
cultured chaps who know everything about everything'. You
can't, at the same time, have a pop-to-*avant garde* approach to a
single subject, and also have a wide range of subjects dealt
with across the board at one level; maybe in the end it was
thought better to dig deeper on individual arts and not try to
make everyone understand the lot of them.

147

But I'm sorry. It *was* a good idea for the theatre critics to be forced to know something about an artist who might be a set designer next; it *was* good for film critics to be made to read books and extremely good for the high-brow to be forced from time to time into low-brow films. For the public it may have been as predictable as the Prayer Book; for us it was a liberal education.

36 · The Risk of Living

Among the posthumous fans of James Dean there was apparently one group that wouldn't believe he was dead. They thought he was disfigured, disabled, hiding: 'Come out, Jamie,' they wrote. 'We still love you – we'll love you whatever you're like.' Statistically they were about right. For as the death figures go down the figures of the half-alive go up. If Hobbes called the life of man nasty, brutish and short, we can say it is one thing worse these days – nasty, brutish and long. And the implications are not quite what you might think.

First you think: 'It ought to be stopped'. Road accidents, now, surely they can be prevented? Half the world thinks that safer roads and cars would do it, the other half that people won't behave sanely in cars till you straighten out human psychology.

As there's an equally fat hope of either, we can take it that accidents will go on. And then what happens? The blood-pump, the resuscitator, the splints and the skin grafts; the body is stitched together again as best it may; the day comes when the doctors push their product out into the world again.

But a pretty bleak world it can be, seen from a wheelchair or from behind a face that makes people look quickly away. It's worst of all for the ones with brain damage, that Jonathan Miller called 'the Rip Van Winkles of science fiction who wake to find themselves unemployable vegetables – thick-tongued, slow-speaking spastics who may have a whole lifetime still before them.'

Does this make you rage at the irresponsible doctors? That's hardly the point; for when you snatch someone from the jaws of death there's often no way of knowing how much is left; you can only cure half the people by risking half-curing the rest. With some doctor-induced illnesses, like thalidomide or the kind of blindness you got while they were still pumping too much oxygen into premature babies, you could make the trade a scapegoat; and maybe the spina bifida problem is still in the doctor's hands – babies born at the rate of sixty a week with a split spine and the nerves exposed. Ten years ago they mostly died in a year or two; now a series of operations brings a third of them up to school age – but more than half are pretty severely handicapped. Should the doctors have operated? 'Any good parent would settle happily even for a crippled condition – even for a short life' – but have we the right to sentence a child to nine years' pain to satisfy parental feelings? I don't know; I only know this isn't the sort of problem you can solve by rule of thumb.

All we can say is that the Safe Society is a myth: the regular risks go on. Industrial ones: you make the best boots and helmets in the world and the chaps won't necessarily wear them – I remember a man who came to throw acid over some stone in our garden who refused his mask and goggles even after he'd had a day's illness from the fumes. Military ones: in theory we don't have wars any more, of course – except that this country has had ninety-three military involvements since 1945 – and the soldiers reckon on five wounded for every one killed. Drugs bring the old folks round again for another ten years of fumbling and neglect; they have no grand deathbed scenes, but fade away slowly in confusion; in the midst of life we are in – life.

On any problem the standard solution is to shriek for more social provision – more workshops, better hostels, closer community care. Great stress is laid these days on the propping power of the peer group – widows huddle with widows, alcoholics get together; but the blind leading the blind are hardly more heartbreaking than that club for 'lame brains' they showed recently on television: they sang 'We shall overcome' very slowly, and everyone knew they couldn't, not on their own. Certainly we could do something to stop the young chronic sick from being dumped in geriatric wards, or keep the lame brains out of places for the mentally deranged; but even if they were all correctly sorted, nurse care for life in a room with thirty beds is not much of a design for living.

More to the point, there's far too little that helps people carry on at home. You read the cases: the single woman coping with an old and dotty mother who asks only for a few days a year away from the grumbling and the wetting; or the woman with an autistic child who could keep going disproportionately better if she had even one afternoon a week to get out and do her own shopping. You hear of the husband who comes home from work and looks after his handicapped wife and all her normal chores; it makes a strange contrast to the magazine chat about staying young and beautiful if you want to keep your man. Sometimes one feels it's the family that needs help more than the patient: 'Whenever I hear of a disabled person doing wonderfully,' says Miss Norwood of the Central Council for the Disabled, 'I look over their shoulder for the worn face in the background – the second line in the fight.'

– So the family is the source of all our discontents, Dr Leach? How lucky that those are the only sort of discontents you have known – or do you suppose that you'd be just as welcome at King's College High Table with a mental age of eight? So the conventional bonds are outdated and artificial, Marianne Faithfull? Let us hope, then, that when you have your babies none of them turns out to need the round-the-clock care a spastic might want. Of course in your case money might help – but how many other women could cope, maybe alone, with the father a lover till something do us part? The family may be a restrictive tool of the capitalist society, as they say at the LSE, or a dead drag on Carnaby Street – but whose swinging friends go on slogging round to see them in hospital, after the first few years?

'One would be in less danger from the wiles of the stranger,' sang Ogden Nash, 'if one's own kin and kith were more fun to be with.' But families aren't for fun. They're an insurance policy against the hazards of living. We simply kid ourselves if we think the hazards of living have stopped; we need our families as much as ever we did. Those who think they don't had better be lucky. They'd better not go in fast cars, or stand too near the edge of the pavement. They had better not develop weak hearts, or have babies that grow with weak brains. And above all they should take care not to grow old.

37 · Getting Your Own Back

P. G. WODEHOUSE has the theory that much modern literature springs from the practice of putting shiny white tiles in lavatories: deprived of their natural medium, he feels, the *graffiti* writers have been forced to take to print. He could be wrong; but there's no denying the escape-valve value of a little direct action, of which writing things on walls is only a small part.

The man who wrote on a hoarding in Kilburn 'Psychiatry Kills' would no doubt have been applauded by his analyst for getting it off his chest so neatly – and I say 'man', for the natural weapon of women is lipstick. In a ladies room I saw recently a disgusting rag of towel hung from a broken machine that was surmounted by a pious notice saying 'NOW WASH YOUR HANDS'; a lipsticked message on the towel-holder said 'NOW WASH THE TOWEL'. And I've heard, though I'm not sure I believe it, that a jilted girl once got back into the arms of her beach hero just long enough to write a rude word on his torso in instant suntan. Well, not quite instant: took about five hours to develop. And there was the case of the outraged lord who went and picnicked on the suburban front lawn of his trespassers – *he* got his own back at least.

What do you *do* when you want to savage people and can't? If your taxi-driver says women drivers and/or Negroes ought to be shot, and you think in a free society people shouldn't be penalized for their opinions, you can't very well not tip him; there's nothing to stop you paying him in pennies, though. A bad shop charges sixpence for a small carrier bag with their advertising all over it; well, one reader of mine says he laboriously turns it inside out as they sit there holding out his change. Another man got so tired of getting incorrect bills from a certain Great Store he simply tore them in half and sent the bits back until they got it right; and another, roused by a neighbour's party, diabolically waited until the last guest had called a gay goodbye at four in the morning, and *then* got his daughter up to do her piano practice.

I have enormous sympathy with the man, a builder by trade, who filled his wife's lover's red sports car with concrete. But even if he hadn't, in fact, picked the wrong car (the lover came out of the house and peacefully bicycled away), I fear it was not really on. Personal Direct Action revenges the crimes that are beneath the notice of the law, and should not get to the point of real damage. Hand a local bigwig a potato at some moment of maximum dignity by all means, but do not remove a plank from the platform so that he falls through and breaks a leg.

The perfect piece of PDA has two characteristics: the victims must know *why* they are being got at, and no guilt must mar our own pure triumph. This is why almost all motoring revenge is out: re-overtaking the man who cut in and then staying on the crown of the road is dangerous, because you may madden the man into overtaking blind; only in the parking lot does the lipstick – for use on the windows of cars that have boxed you in – come safely into its own again.

Journalists can get their own back on public figures for boring them to death simply by printing every word they say – Eisenhower in the States got a fair amount of 'I am, of course, very interested – ah – to hear that, because as you know I'm very interested ... um ... er ... but in the circumstances, as things are ... ah ... I know you would not expect me to be definite at this time.'

154

And some trifling Fleet Street score was once settled in a manner that has become a classic. One man rang up a distinguished foreign editor late one night and, imitating the Scottish voice of the night editor, said they'd heard the French Government had fallen, and there were instructions that there was to be a leader on it. Naturally not wishing to reveal that this took him totally by surprise, the foreign editor said, 'Ah, yes, I was expecting this,' put the phone down and frantically rang Paris. The Paris correspondent, roused from a warm bed, wasn't going to admit that this was the first he'd heard of it either, so he nodded as sagely as you can nod over the long-distance telephone, and then started ringing round all the other correspondents, most of whom behaved in exactly the same way. Finally, of course, someone rang the Elysée and the gaff was blown. The point is that this one would never have got to the point where the news was printed, an international crisis was provoked and the man lost his job. That would have been cheating.

I imagine a lot of people will feel all this is playing with fire, that it's one step away from Sicilian vendettas, guns, vigilantes and mob rule. But I think it might work the other way round. We all suffer so much from the enormous frustration of feeling we can't *do* anything about the things that madden us: about the machines that go wrong or the supplier that is rude or the MP who talks nonsense. But if you can keep on delivering dead flowers to the managing director's office, or get someone to fiddle the mike so that your MP speaks now in a whisper, now in a thunderous roar, I think you might keep off the real excesses. You would be less tempted to shout down the MP or burn down the firm or build up your rage to the point where you sink your flick knife into the upholstery.

If a man beats you to an empty seat, which is fair, and smiles smugly, which isn't, he is bound to get banged a bit by the shopping bags it is so hard to hold standing up. If a mother is kept waiting too long, she has a perfect right to apply the ultimate deterrent and release the children – and if the man down the road won't curb *his* small boy, you could always make the lad a present of a trumpet. . . .

38 · The Daily Round

If, you too, spend bank holiday weekends yawning your way through the predictability of the 'news' stories, you certainly have my sympathy. But the papers get that way not just because, as the *Observer* office notice board once remarked, 'Everyone seems to want to visit their grandmothers in Iceland over the holiday'; there really are fewer hard stories around. No courts; so no judges describing as 'the wear and tear of married life' the man who counts out the housekeeping in farthings or the woman who starches his socks. No Parliament, no late-night sittings and so none of the splendid indiscretions brought on by lack of sleep. And the closure of the banks plus the departure of every financier to his weekend *Schloss* means we can't even have a monetary crisis – one wonders why they don't do it oftener. We are reduced to the basic slag of news stories, the sure-fire perennials; and that being the case I don't see why we shouldn't ensure ourselves some extra holiday by writing the next bank holiday's news stories now.

There are, to start with, the straight holiday stories. TRAFFIC JAM AROUND EXETER is a dead cert, and if you set up both HOLIDAY CROWDS THRONG BEACHES and RAIN SOAKS HOLIDAY CROWDS you're safe (nobody, of course, knows whether it has been raining or not until the papers say). The road casualties will be either marginally up or marginally down, so either it's SAFER HOLIDAY ON ROADS or DEATH TOLL MOUNTS.

Politicians, who spend holidays out in the constituencies saying the right thing, can be simply dealt with by a permutation series: HEATH ATTACKS WILSON, SUMMERSKILL ATTACKS HEATH, WILSON ATTACKS CALLAGHAN, MACLEOD ATTACKS POWELL – and of course there's always BRITAIN NOW TENTH-RATE POWER, SAYS COL. BLEECHER. Prince Philip goes about his business as the nation's rough bath towel, to Brace without actually Hurting; and one can determine whether it's to be PRINCE PHILIP'S CALL TO INDUSTRY or PRINCE PHILIP'S CALL TO STUDENTS simply by consulting the royal diary in advance. I have been skipping for fifteen years all headlines beginning GENEVA PEACE TALKS BREAK DOWN/STALEMATE/REOPEN without having missed a thing – I just hope to God VIETNAM PEACE TALKS is not going the same way. By now no one reads beyond the headline LSE STUDENTS IN REVOLT. Nor do we, finger to text, lips eagerly moving, go line by line down anything headed UNION REJECTS OFFER or CBI CONDEMNS INDUSTRIAL PROPOSALS; so for all these we can write up any old story for the bank holiday issue and get away with it.

The Church is apt to be frustrating to journalists, since the best remarks of their best men are usually too violent to print. For our standard headlines, therefore, we fall back on VICAR MET VERGER'S WIFE IN CRYPT, or the puritans who refuse their services to people who don't come to church, as in VICAR REFUSES BAPTISM: the story following always indicates a high degree of huff on the part of the parents: 'We had it all planned and thirty people invited.'

CURATE ATTACKS COURTING COUPLES is one of my favourites, even although it always turns out (just as you picture him sneaking down lover's lane with an axe) that he has merely passed some remarks in the parish magazine. Best of all is the swinging vicar who conducts a motor-cycle rally in the grave-yard, invites the Rolling Stones to tea or advertises a pray-in with electric guitars. For him, a limerick: There was a young Vicar of Twynge, Who courted the lunatic fringe. As he danced down the nave, Crying 'Man, it's a rave, This communion's a real way-out binge' – they always do get the slang at least half wrong.

Except for the beach shots, I'm not sure how forehanded we can be with pictures. There's the Queen in a headscarf looking worried about a horse, of course, and there's usually a pathetic puppy on account of whom some couple is being evicted – the fourteen large Alsatians they also keep not usually getting into the picture. The two hairy hippies who go with the recurrent POP STAR ON DRUGS CHARGE could probably be reproduced *ad infinitum*, but even the bathing beauties show different amounts from different angles every year, and fashion, of course, can hardly be more than a few weeks old. It's not that the *clothes* change particularly; but the fashions in illustration certainly do: pairs of girls in lesbian poses one month, dwarf paper dolls in gritty little rows the next, elongated inside thighs to follow. In a trade where shoving the lens a further two inches up the crotch counts as originality, a photographer is caught with last month's fad at his peril.

The headlines which you can set in advance and build up from almost anything are the really startling ones like ALL BABIES BORN IN TEST TUBES SOON or FLYING CARS BY 1980. When you read on it becomes: 'By 1980 we shall all have to walk or have cars that fly if nothing is done about the present state of congestion on our roads,' said Professor Abel Semen, speaking at the Regional Tarmac Operators' conference at Grimsby this weekend.

And whatever else fails, we can always count on the council. 'HOUSES PERFECTLY SATISFACTORY,' SAYS COUNCILLOR JONES of the Housing Committee, commenting on the complaint by two tenants of the Manor Lane estate that their roofs blew off in last week's gale. 'Some people will use any excuse to complain, but I for one am not going to waste rate-payers' money on frivolous redecorations.' Only the farmer who last week wanted to discourage dogs from worrying sheep by putting up the cost of their licences came anywhere near the usual joyous 'MOTORWAYS SHOULD BE ABOLISHED,' SAYS COUNCILLOR PERKS.

The really sickening thing, of course, is that all these incessant stories are true – it's not our fault that we cannot stun you with something like GOLDFISH EATS OWNER, CHINA JOINS COMMON MARKET or POHER SEDUCES POMPIDOU. It would almost be worth the Newspaper Publishers' Association paying a man to bite a dog – except, of course, for the long, predictable fuss there'd be from the RSPCA.

39 · Models Make Good

A sleek body, a beautiful way of moving, even if it's combined with a lot of get-up-and-go is not enough to make a great name in films. The essential ingredient is subtler, harder to come by: the star quality that will have men breathless, women in tears and children mouse-trapped in their tip seats with excitement. Does the new name in Twentieth-Century Fox's forthcoming production – 'Hello and Goodbye' – have it?

This correspondent answers with a resounding yes. She has good looks, momentum, more than 1500 cc and a top speed of 120 mph; and if she lacks the gadgets that have sent the James Bond Aston Martin and Chitty Chitty Bang Bang into a million homes in model form, she has something else – ambition. To Lotus Elan, to be one more rising carlet is not enough; she means to *act*.

'It had to come,' she said when I interviewed her in her Apicella garage under the Dorchester. 'It's like male ballet dancers – for years they were nothing more than a prop to the ballerina, then suddenly they started to be something in their own right. Human-dominated films are *out*, thank goodness; now it's a question of what we can make of our great chance.'

Not that Miss Elan is blindly uncritical of the car films that have been made so far. 'Of course the Yellow Rolls-Royce is an absolute trouper and a darling personality, but did it do us any good – in the long run, I mean – to have a film built round someone who, let's face it, *is* getting on a bit? "Monte Carlo or Bust" had some good moments, and I suppose we

L 161

have to go through that cliff-hanging stage the way the old silent films had to, but honestly, what did the hanging-over-the-river bit do that Charlie Chaplin in the "Gold Rush" hadn't done with his shack? And the personalities – I suppose it's all part of this fad for the anti-hero or something – all those provincial faces and exhaust noises – you've got to admit there wasn't a real Bentley among them.'

She stresses, though, that she is not a snob. 'Look, we all know it's the age of the common car; I'm not pretending I was hand-tooled by, I mean for, Prince Chula of Beaulieu or anything. Style's a matter of personality, don't you think? Look at that ravishing little German who played Herbie in "The Love Bug". He's one of my greatest personal friends: I do think small cars can have very great appeal – like James Cagney on wheels or – or – James Cagney.

'That was a great movie he made; though of course they had to put a slushy ending on it to please the box office. It's supposed to be a secret but I don't mind telling *you* [and my four million readers] that it should have ended with the human couple rolling over and over down a cliff, breaking up in flames; Herbie was to be looking out into the sunset – he'd have won an Oscar for that scene. That really gets me, I mean spoiling a film for the sake of what happens to the people in them – enough cars get killed just for thrills after all.

'Of course I suppose that's really why we've got our break in films now. People like a forbidden kick at the cinema. It used to be sex; but now nothing is forbidden much, people mostly do what they like; the producers make it more and more way out, but if it isn't kinky in your way, what's the draw?

'But there's no permissiveness with motors. People want to drive their cars down the steps of museums and across rivers, they want to crash the car next to them and go round on two wheels, to let us – you know – *give*; but they can't do it. The police won't let them, the insurance companies won't let them, it's probably the company car anyway, they have to be careful. When that man in "Bullitt", I forget his name, drove the Ford Mustang down the hills of San Francisco bouncing into sight like a ski-jumper, that was a release for a whole generation of kids who wanted to do just that.

'Mind you, I think they take it too far – all that mangled metal, petrol spilt all over the road, all those cars burning and falling to pieces in "The Italian Job", it's just pointless sadism, I can't watch stuff like that. Anyway, those Minis – well, they're very sweet girls and I always stand up for them when people say how terribly boring they are; but they don't exactly have – what's the word – car-isma, do they?

'What really riles me are the people who say we're just machines, we don't have feelings. Why, the first great car part was a romantic lead, wasn't it? "Genevieve", making the wife jealous – it's a pure love triangle. She was absolutely splendid, wasn't she – though I gather the director had to be terribly, terribly patient with her: well, if you were Juliet's nurse playing Cleopatra you wouldn't fire on six all the time, would you?

'And those people who think we're just demure little bits of machinery – well, they ought to come to a private showing we're having next week, that's all: there's one scene where this man is stripping down his car, very slowly, very cold. . . . I tell you, we had one character who just couldn't stand it, had to go out. He had terrible problems, anyway, I admit – started on Redex and then couldn't keep off the shots . . . finally had to join the A.A.'

For her own tastes, I gather Miss Elan doesn't go for the bulldozer type: 'All those sweaty lorries in the "Wages of Fear" – it's not my scene, dear, no. And that car transporter in "The Italian Job" – well, really, six cars at a time, no thank you.' She admitted, her huge headlights misting for a moment, that she hadn't yet found what she was looking for – there have been no great villains in car films yet. 'But I'm hoping,' she says. 'And when he comes, he'll be no dumb truck, I can tell you that. When all's said and done you do like to be – er – co-starred with someone where you can hear the clock tick no matter how fast he's going.'

40 · Who Wrote You?

When you see a hunted figure shuffling past on the far side of the street with his collar turned up, it is probably an author avoiding the friends who say, 'Are you putting me in your book?' Most authors deny doing this, at least at all directly; but few of them own up to the opposite fact: that they actually *make* the characters they write about.

Were there any Lucky Jims before Amis wrote them? I never heard of one; but afterwards you couldn't drop cigarette-ash anywhere without it falling into the floppy turn-ups of provincial *débrouillards*. They just crawled off the page and started making faces. Was there a real Lord Jim? He is certainly the way to carry on if you have that sort of Shame, but before? (you will remember poor Thurber, going round the Pacific being Lord Jim: they tried to sell him baskets).

Irish girls used to come over to England and, dropping the brogue and the wee girl bit as they stepped off the night packet, get absorbed in the surrounding scene with tolerably little fuss. Now, more's the pity, they stick it out as Edna O'Brien girls, wearing little bits of swansdown at parties and sleeping with people in a fit of absence of mind. Nobody really supposes that John Updike looked out at his coupling neighbours and simply wrote down what they were up to; but I bet they're up to it now – and heaven knows what happens when the suburban sprawl reaches out into the East Anglian fastness of Akenfield and Peter Grimes – they'll be having brother-swapping parties next.

For a time I was puzzled by the number of vulnerable, sensitive women you see now and then vaguely blinking in shops: these curious creatures, born with one skin too few, on whom everything reacts with the psychedelic intensity of a screen too close to the projector. Surely they were around long before the Pumpkin Eater's wife went off her head in Harrods, before even the marine Venuses of Margaret Drabble, who surface into normal humdrum life about once per book? That was when I hadn't taken it in that fashionable Jean Rhys was, in fact, writing about the great non-copers of all time in the thirties: obviously, after leaving Mr Mackenzie they just drifted off on the loose and are with us still.

This is not the same as the effects of books or TV on existing people – lawyers going bankrupt because they can't produce a surprise witness in every case like Perry Mason, or ex-future directors blustering like Patrick Wymark. It's creation I'm talking about: those splendid low-key self-contained single women made by Margery Sharp (who without her would hardly exist at all since the breeding of Sister George); the J. B. Priestley, Margaret Kennedy men – all walking and pipes and open-necked shirts; or, conversely, that whole race of elegant fellows, pronouncing each syllable and holding wine-glasses by the stem, whose totem is still, deep down, Sebastian's teddy bear, Aloysius.

The great country houses of P. G. Wodehouse (surely never made by any human hand without a pen in it) would have collapsed utterly by now if they hadn't been rewritten among the introspective cobwebs of Ivy Compton Burnett. Some authors, of course, are reduced to writing themselves: I once asked William Haggard to pull out a couple of corks for me and he said 'Oh yes, I think Colonel Russell can decant claret'; but mostly it's categories they make – the real source of the population problem is too many books.

At the moment, the sexual spree celebrating the lifting of the taboos means that there are six works investigating the problems of an Oedipal inverted tripartite relationship for every one person actually afflicted with this; when the reaction inevitably comes (even theatre audiences will one day cry 'Don't just stand, do something!') their numbers may well be up to the things written about them.

Ronald Bryden says he comes out of Henry James – the New Worlder in search of old-world culture; my most miserable friend is plainly straight out of the *Last Exit to Brooklyn*. The cleverest man I know (well, second cleverest, I don't want to get into a fight) reveals himself to be Stephen Dedalus; if the solid fellow is really a stream of consciousness inside it explains a great deal.

I attribute my sunny state to the fact that I was written by American ladies of the early 1900s who wrote about glad college girls who marry, after a fantastic amount of chat, the men of their dreams. And you only have to look around you to see that the people written by Jane Austen are more cheerful than those written by George Eliot, and break fewer things round the house than the products of any Brontë.

It seems to me this is a much handier method of adding people up than the usual inquiry into whether they were breast-fed, went to a bad public school, have a low IQ or the XY chromosome – better even than the background inquiry of Betty Macdonald's 'Have you or any of your family ever had Bright's disease, TB, epilepsy, a steady job, etc., etc.?' Everybody was written by somebody; and as for the unique individualist you can't place – he's simply had the luck to be out of a book that nobody else has read.

41 · You Can Say That Again

Not many people go around using the word 'Guevarism' to mean the over-elaborate prose style favoured by the six-teenth-century poet of that name; but young modern slang on the lips of anyone over twenty-five is often just about as dated. It is far safer, to my mind, to cheer up a sagging vocabulary by digging up the floorboards for forgotten relics.

The words are right there waiting. 'Gibbetation' would be a much better euphemism for the advocates of 'capital punishment' – matches the date on their thinking, too. Those who hit the headlines by coming to life again have undergone 'reviction'; and when you don't know how to put it when he's married the girl he once divorced, you can call her his resumptive wife. If you hate 'toddler' and are sick of 'kid', you can call a small child a kinchin – it sounds like a baby-wear brand already; and if you don't want to say 'old bean' or 'old chap' lest you cut your clean young English throat on your clean English collar, say 'Come on, old gloak', instead – it only means man, after all.

Devious fun can be had with words which are still around, but used to have entirely different meanings – 'fun' itself meant cheat, and a fun-loving wench was simply a crook. 'Presently' used to mean 'at once' – I like to think of the centuries and centuries of people not getting up and doing it right away that has led the word to its current meaning. 'En-thusiasm' was once reserved for those who thought they had a private revelation from the Almighty; 'delicate' once meant something much more like 'delicious' (which gives a quite different light on lexicographer Francis Grose talking about the delicate parts of a woman); I'd love to hear someone turning down some proposed treat with the words 'No, it's indelicate' - meaning only that it wouldn't give pleasure. 'Rude' once just meant rough or countrified, and 'nice' particular or exact or scrupulous: if you told Dr Johnson the story about the girl asked how she liked marriage, who said 'Oh it's nice, but isn't it rude?' he wouldn't know what on earth you meant.

Words meaning poor or ordinary are always apt to go down the scale. Just as you say 'don't be a guttersnipe' to your messy offspring, so 'naughty' meant first poor, then bad, then - naughty. 'Vulgar' used to mean the vernacular before it meant rhinestones and plastic; 'common' was the noble commune until it got to the sentence 'they have nothing in common except that they both are'. Words gain or lose a sexual context - 'friend' has gone from lover to friend back to its current equivocal sense, and 'intercourse' once meant social intercourse, which makes hilarious reading of seminary brochures promising the young ladies just that.

Hating the word because you hate the tone it's spoken in is a wider subject; but the unmarried mothers, now as tired of 'illegitimate' as they once were of 'bastard', recently suggested they go back to the phrase 'natural child' - except that it suggests all the others are unnatural. And you can revive ideas - or at least get them into the argument - just by bringing back the words: 'homewrecker', for instance, or 'gluttony'; 'philosophy' in its sense of 'knowledge' or 'modesty' - what *is* modesty anyway besides not sitting with your legs apart in trains? There must surely be more to it than that.

If you said that Nicholas Tomalin, who took the lid off the wine trade, went caterwauling after balderdash he'd likely sue, but caterwauling can mean smelling out an intrigue, and balderdash was adulterated wine. Interview is a laughable word these days – but you could call the victim the 'opinator', the one who has opinions, and the hatchet man the 'oppugner' – the one who opposes or attacks. Call an eating house 'The Squill and Quiddle' and they'd doubtless all pack in – not knowing that squill's an all but inedible vegetable, and quiddle meant spit, till it understandably came to be applied to boarding-school custard.

In the riotous society 'know' has practically resumed its seventeenth-century meaning of 'go to bed with'. It's amazing we haven't revived 'enjoy' in its 'Dutch Courtesan' sense of 'I must enjoy her!' or the word 'framp' meaning to revel in something: though it's understandable that we use less the quiet little word 'grubble', which means to feel for something in the dark. 'Dead Chelsea!', of course, was something you exclaimed as your leg was shot away in battle, meaning you'd end up in that village near London famous for its hospital; it was then frequented by old fogeys, the furious ones, and not by those whom the fogeys would doubtless have regarded as beginners and fops – the eriffs and the fribbles. They would not be surprised to know that 'permissive' comes from the Latin word for surrender; but do they know that in the thirteenth century 'girl' meant either a maiden or a youth?

I don't know whether the old words are ever really stronger than the ones you know; they just feel that way. When Sydney Smith talks about 'the gripe of reason' it seems tougher, grittier than just keeping your grip; I don't know how we managed without being able to say 'Mop up that spilth at once'. 'Gallied' means harried like a galley-slave, and before it had anything to do with freezing, the word 'fridge' meant shifting restlessly around.

And how about 'squab', which is how a tortoise sounds when it's dropped from a height by an eagle, when used to describe a girl – 'that man and his squab daughter'.

Lewis Carroll and John Lennon make up their own words, but most of us are too gallied with the kinchin fridging about in the spilth to have time. But at least we can always bring in the old word to redress the balance of the new.

42 · All the World's a Toy

Up and down the steep streets of Brighton drive the decorated minibuses; girls in red skirts and frozen smiles hand out pamphlets for Skipoo (hula-hoop to you); half the hotel rooms in towns have turned into Aladdin's caves glowing with tinsel and jigsaws, bicycles and fireworks and bears. 'No Children Allowed', says a notice and quite right too: they are always in the way when grown-ups want to play. Then what are those little cowgirls doing riding their metal horses down the corridor? They are demonstration girls, says the Toy Fair man sternly, assessing me for size, and no, I cannot try the horses myself. The hell with him; there is a car on another stand that takes them up to 150 lb; it goes backwards and forwards on a battery until I finally come to my senses.

Of course the toy trade is always explaining that it is fierce and competitive and in constant danger from American takeovers; but somehow cheerfulness keeps on breaking in. There are so many family firms – the Spears, the Dol-Toi people (everything for the doll's house), the genial Cassidy brothers who make model washing-machines and are first cousins to the last editor of the *New Statesman*. They all know one another, they all come every year, and at least it isn't Harrogate, thank God. *That* is for the wholesale trade and, as if just being in Harrogate wasn't enough, it happens during the Christmas hangover period. 'Why don't we make a trade fair kit?' I asked one man. 'Stalls, little stuffed men in navy suits, toy toys?' 'Mine would be a bottle of Fernet Branca and some aspirins,' he said.

It must be admitted they do pinch one another's ideas; on

some stands they practically strip you to the bone to make sure you say 'Press' all the way through. There are three rival plastic car tracks, two sets of interlocking blocks, two 'poseable' dolls at least – one 'as poseable as you are' – you mean I can bend my arm back at right angles from the elbow? You can usually tell the imitator by the high querulous tone in which he explains why his is the better product.

There's another sameness too, a mid-Atlantic look: white shoes for nurses, freckles, Dune Buggies seen by the British child only on the Cliff Richard programme. It's not that they're all designed in America, but to keep prices down toys must sell in a lot of countries (a global *model* village, yet). Toy cars, too: a Rolls is known and sells everywhere, but they don't make Aston Martins unless James Bond helps the publicity. Toy firms get new car designs well ahead of the public; if I were an industrial spy I'd spend my time hanging about a toy factory disguised as a stuffed elephant. *And* I know what eyes I'd choose: they come in six standard styles, Amber, Blue, Pink, Tortoiseshell, Cat's and Character.

There is still plenty of business through small shops, not just supermarkets, which makes it still a trade where newcomers can break in – the Petratoy people, for example, who make one of the best and cheapest cardboard playhouses, or a fancy-dress designer who used to design for the stage. The toyshop people are in two minds about the effects of TV advertising and TV characters like Dougal and Sooty: they boost sales at the time but are dead as Mutt and Jeff a few weeks too late. Maybe they should try more durable types like the Muggeridge Doll (weeps and prays) or the Robin Day (his tie lights up when you cringe).

Whether the toys are for children or grown-ups seems less clear every year, and I don't mean the cliché about Dads and toy trains. The science sets need a more and more advanced small boy, half the model stuff is in fact bought by men and they tell you with tears in their eyes that the painting by numbers is only for housewives, really it is. Lovable woolly toys are aimed at grandmothers, because that's how they feel about babies: I was relieved to hear it, for we have the greatest collection of unloved fluffy animals in London – God, what Des Wilson would make of their plight; other children, too, it seems, prefer to curl up with a truck.

Adult preference – three parts nostalgia to one of Good Taste – may in fact be the needed brake on the transitory gimmick trade. Ah, how we wound ourselves up in our raffia! Oh, the Monopoly and the Meccano and the weaving machine, the bear that had its appendix operated on so often it was only fit to be the corpse in a gunfight! If the little ones, we say sniffing into our pink Kleenex, want their Matt Mason and their Noddy Cut-outs they can jolly well buy them themselves.

But there's nothing like a day among the rich roaring commerce of the Toy Fair to weary one of the worthiness of things like the Consumer Council's pamphlet on toy buying or the British Toymakers' Guild. All right, it's crazy to pay a lot for a limited toy if you haven't got a lot, and safety counts. But just how does one follow the council's advice to ask the assistant, 'Will the toy last until all its play possibilities have been exhausted?' They're exhausted anyway when it's smashed.

They don't approve of kits that show you too closely what the finished result should be; and no doubt such kits provide only what, given a few Squeezy bottles, some glue, ingenuity and two hours to spare, you could set up yourself. But how often is it *you*, not the child, who has to do all that? I feel like Cyril Ray and bottling your own wine: he explained how you could save 6d a bottle by this great process, and then admitted that if anyone came and offered to do it all for him for only 6d he'd weep with relief. Huge plush horses may be a guilty father's last throw on Christmas Eve – but who wants those static gingham animals the crafters make, either? A friend of mine bought a great Pooh for his son; neighbours hid it for him, and on Christmas Day they stationed it outside the door, rang the bell and went away. Far too big, no doubt. A weak commercial gimmick, OK – but I bet the child got something out of it all the same. The one thing the worthies forget is that to a child everything is a toy – even toys.

43 · Mistakes of the Season

A man once said he knew it was time to get up when he heard his wife scraping the burnt toast; and quite bitter he sounded when he said it, too. I know how he feels; it's not the mistakes people make – it's not even one's own mistakes – that really get one down; it's the fact that we go on making the same mistakes over and over again. And the Christmas ones seem peculiarly inescapable.

It's the optimism that causes it, I suppose – and there's nothing so seasonal about that. All the year round we go on gamely believing that we'll remember addresses without writing them down, that the mini-cab will actually turn up, that there'll be time in the morning. Red must come up next time, it will be all right on the night, the Lord will provide.

Every Christmas we follow the same cycle. This year, we say, we won't overdo it, won't overspend, won't knock ourselves out. There will be nothing but peace and children's voices through the frosty air and a few small presents ready-wrapped round the tree; this year at least we shall cook a really very straightforward meal without getting into a towering flap. But come Christmas Eve, we are crawling over the carpet wrapping presents while the voices of the better organized boom from the Midnight Mass across the street; on Christmas morning the children may be waiting round the piano but we are still peering desperately into the yawning maw of the unstuffed turkey, tempted, as with a gas-oven, to put one's head into it and sob.

But why? I have a nasty feeling that those of us for whom this sort of chaos is a way of life must somehow be doing it to satisfy an unconscious need. If we get into a great scramble over Christmas, it may be that we like to feel like a general in the centre of battle; he may not know what's going on but, by God, he's indispensable.

I tell myself, too, that we always could get it straight if we really cared enough. Fundamentally the people who make lop-sided cakes are not those who think that they will be judged at the bar of heaven on the sides of their cakes; at any rate we excuse our lateness by the other vital things we have to do and the dirt by implying we have creative children. Of course it's always a perfectly genuine accident when things go wrong – but it's funny how they don't when your heart is really in it, just as people who can't wake up for work can always catch an aeroplane on holiday.

Probably, though, our utter inability to learn from experience is as much a matter of memory as anything else. It's the flip side of the merciful oblivion which hides things like childbirth and builders: if one remembered the whole horrible truth one would simply never have the nerve to start again. Look, indeed, at the people who do building for a living: their *déformation professionnelle* is to keep forever the happy optimism of a fresh do-it-yourselfer: it'll only take an evening or two, it won't cost much, there's bound to be some more paper if we run out of this lot. Memory may have held the door for John Buchan; it simply slams it on the fingers of the rest of us.

This year, though, I've outwitted myself – at least on this last score. If I muck it again it will be my own fault, for last January I made a series of disillusioned notes. I am reminding myself, now, that the point of shopping in the first, not the third week in December is not just that there are more and cheaper things, but that the shops will still send. The note says not only that the shops are empty in the early mornings, which I know anyway, but that it is the housewifely conviction that you'd better make the bed before you go out which stops you cashing in on this fact: this year, no bedmaking before noon. I have told myself to keep all the oddments I buy in the same place (instead of finding them around the house after Boxing Day), to wrap as I go to avoid the final madhouse, and to label the things so that I don't have to unwrap them later to find out what they are.

This time, the budget will include the protection racket of milkmen and dustmen (it was sickening, during the strike, I had to call off my personal war with the dustmen for the sake of proletarian solidarity). Under no provocation shall I buy all those dates and nuts and slices which only serve to keep you eating right on into January. And the little ones can tear their grandmothers' hearts out with their own constructions of paint and paper instead of a horrid, impersonal shop-bought object; you can save pounds that way.

Much the best way of solving the food question is to go and stay with someone else. Otherwise, the list says lay off lunch if the turkey is in the evening – why *not* just sausages on sticks and ice-cream and cheese? And as for peeling the sprouts – well, I'm all for fresh foods for festivals, but any taste sprouts have is objectionable; so why not have frozen ones and be grateful there's much less of it?

The main thing to remember is that however good your Christmas, there always tends to be too much of it. It goes on too long, it costs too much, you feel blown out: the opposite of a merry Christmas is surfeit. And nowhere is this worse than surfeit of presents – you go on unwrapping as different relatives arrive and somehow never seem to get over that stage and get on with Christmas itself. Fewer presents all round (it's a question of number and fuss as much as cost) and I bet we'd enjoy it far more.

Ask anybody about their favourite Christmas and you usually get told about the one during the war when we made decorations out of fir cones, or that year we were broke and presents not from Woolworth's were forbidden. In the most tear-jerking of the lot, the one in *Little Women*, they gave away their breakfast, and the ending of *A Christmas Carol* was mainly happy because they'd been starving all week and not lushing it up at office parties. The one thing that really needs remembering is that it's the attempt to blow the balloon too big that results in the limp rag at the end.

44 · Grub on Offer

I don't know if it's going to be all right – I mean, it's just
something I thought of doing. . . .

You know it'll be lovely, Timothy, it always is.

Yes, well, I think I got the pasta right – I *did* make that myself – but the filling was a recipe I heard on television, I may
not have got everything down.

It's delicious. Now do tell me, what *is* it you're working on
just now?

Oh, this book. But I wonder – I think the filling should have
been cooked a bit more, don't you? Hold on – perhaps a bit
more pepper. . . .

It's FINE. What did you make of 'La Grotesque' at the Film
Festival?

I liked the basic idea, but I thought it was a terribly self-
indulgent piece of direction, he shouldn't have – look, you
don't have to eat it if you don't want to, it was just something
that occurred to me; just a minute, I'd better look at the
soufflé. . . .

*   *   *

Oh Carol, darling, how marvellous – *green* biscuits. What *did*
you put in them?

Butter and sugar and flour and milk and the blue colouring
Mummy gave us, only it turned green, Mummy said it was
because the mixture was yellow, and we tried blue paint-
water but it didn't make any difference – aren't you going to
finish it?

*   *   *

Now, what for you? I think we've got all the usual things: whisky and soda, fine. Oh, blast, I don't think there's any soda made. You would? You're sure you'd just as soon have gin and tonic? I'll just get a case of tonics from the garage . . . look, this is awful, but we seem to have run out of tonics, it's all bitter lemon . . . here you are, then – oh, would you have liked ice?

*   *   *

No potatoes? But surely *you* don't need to diet?

You should see what I look like when I don't – Hattie Jacques isn't in it.

Well, just as you say, of course. I sometimes think of going on a diet myself but with my work I simply do need the energy . . . yes, of course, you do too, but I feel just drained if I don't eat. And you remember Chris Peter-Tomkins, she lost two stone and now she looks as if she'd been struck by lightning . . . are you *sure* you won't have just a little? Go on – after all, men like fat women, don't they?

*   *   *

Once upon a time there was a little boy called – open your mouth – Jake. And one morning he said he didn't want his egg and his Mummy said . . .

*   *   *

Another helping?

No, thanks; it's very nice, but . . .

Oh, I'm so glad you like it – everybody does. You'd never guess what it is, actually: it's just tinned rice pudding – I get them on offer from Tesco's – and a spot of Marmite and peanut butter and a lump of marge. It goes an amazingly long way – actually I invented it, though I say it as shouldn't – I never bother with recipes. . . .

Ah, the vino – that's great: tip it in there. We've had brandy and tonic and beer so far but no wine yet – the spices and orange and stuff's in already, of course. The only way to see they all get sloshed at the same rate, I always say. Pass me that mug, will you – came free with the Fairy Liquid, that did; the wife said that's the only liquid that won't end up in the punch, ha-ha-ha, well, *almost* the only liquid. . . .

*　　*　　*

Gravy?

Oh, thanks. As I was saying, when Pétain was dying in the Hôtel Dieu they thought the great picture of the year was going to be—

Bread sauce?

Oh, thanks. They thought the great picture of the year was going to be of him on his deathbed, so they bribed one of the prison nurses 500 francs to—

Game chips?

Oh, thanks—this nurse was supposed to take a picture of Pétain, they had him in a hotel room practising with one of the newspaper staff lying on the bed pretending to be the Marshal—

Cranberry sauce?

Oh, thanks. And they gave him an expensive camera to do it with but then the great day came and Pétain died and he took the picture but he sold it to—

You did have sprouts, did you? Oh, of course – I'm so sorry; what were you saying?

Oh, never mind.

*　　*　　*

That's right, have a good helping – you always were a one for the porridge, weren't you? Do you make it every morning, Linda, or every other day?

At home he never wants anything but black coffee.

Really? How very odd. He did before he was married. I don't know how people stand it, going out without a proper hot breakfast inside them. Now I'll just do your eggs – have some more toast, dear, it's *no* trouble to make more. . . .

*　　*　　*

More wine? No, it's just the stuff from the supermarket. I reckon Harry gets plenty of château-bottled at his City dinners. Anyway, as I was saying, if she *will* keep all her jewels around the house it's hardly surprising they get stolen; I must admit mine spend more time at the bank than they do with me. Did you like the pudding? Yes, all by myself – a packet, of course, but what's the difference? No, I don't cook on the yacht – we have this marvellous pair of Portuguese brothers.

Oh! oh, goodness – no, don't give it another thought – no, no, it's only Dior London – anyway, Nescafé doesn't stain. . . .

*　　*　　*

Takes you back, doesn't it – it's the aroma as much as anything. Yes, it is a curious way of cutting meat really – my husband says they don't *cut* it at all; on the island we used to hear these distant crumps, they were quarrying or something and he always said they were dynamiting the goats. Yes, it's all authentic except that I couldn't get goat's intestines, these are sheep's. . . .

45 · Smelling Out the Facts

If one of these morning I really can't get my eyes open, I think I'll still have a fair idea what's going on, just by twitching my nose. Has he a dirty nappy? Do I smell bacon or the hot butter for scrambled eggs? Has someone left their gum boots on the radiator? Is anybody pungently ironing? And even if I couldn't read 'On June 14th 8th Air Force decided...' I'd know at once from the acrid ashtray that the bastard had been using my desk again.

A cold spring like this one holds back the smells. For a few weeks more it'll be only the indoor ones, pine baths and new magazines, apples cooling in butter, illicit logs in the smoke-free grate, the comforting fug of one's husband's winter jerseys. And then suddenly we'll be hit by a smell of earth and wet bark; there'll be a hint of hyacinth in the air; cars will smell hot inside and butchers unbearable; later there'll be the fresh-cut smell of grass, and the smell of sausages frying out of doors, and wallflowers and sun-heated stone and the cellar smell of very cold white wine. . . . But not, of course, before the whole house has suddenly started to smell of dust, and every decent whiff in the place has been overlaid with Vim and Chemico and wet shammy-leather.

A science fiction story once had it that, before the common cold, we'd all had noses as sensitive as a dog's; then they cured the cold and every violent smell of civilization hammered at us with nightmare intensity. Certainly the artificial smells are getting the upper hand. Kitchens don't smell of celery when it's in the fridge, you can't get the pong of trodden peapod when you buy peas frozen, no fish is allowed to decay in its own good time. If you have a smell of wet dog it may be the hounds of spring on winter's traces, but it's much more likely the dishwasher (I tried changing the powder, but it only made it smell like a different breed of wet dog).

Heaven knows what all this is doing to our nostalgia: *our* childhood picnics smelt of pine needles and damp egg sandwiches and wet stone; but nowadays my children feast off a cheap red plastic tablecloth with the most peculiar smell. Will they in years to come clutch the bench in a plastics lab, overwhelmed with summer memories of golden long ago?

Considering how emotional we all get about smells, it's amazing how little they're taken into account – by hotels and hash-joints, for example. You'd think at least they'd have the sense to avoid those twin stinks of coke and cheap polish that must remind everybody alive of some hostel, hospital or bad boarding-school; but no. I went to an hotel recently that had had the most elaborate face-lift – yet one breath inside and I knew that nothing had really changed: all the ducted air heating had done was to pipe the smell of stale fat more efficiently round the rooms.

George Orwell thought that smell was the ineradicable basis of class hatred in this country; I'd be prepared to trace Douglas Jay's loathing of the Common Market – nothing alien to him is human – back to a dislike of the mere smell of abroad. In a *Guardian* article recently they found that though children of all colours will play happily together, the child who smells has no friends at all. And women can smell oddly at times of the month they don't even know about: why hasn't *New Society* done some survey on the effect of this on (a) marital crack-up, (b) sexual frequency and (c) the rate of refusal to answer females researching for *New Society*?

It's all even more sinister when you realize there are psychological factors involved in smelling awful, if only because you heat up worse when you're nervous. We had a girl in this office some years ago who ponged something awful: 'They say even your best friends won't tell you,' she said, 'but my best friends tell me *all the time*.' Yet a few weeks later, when she was happily settled, the air became quite breathable again.

And I had a boy friend once who washed like mad but to no avail; maybe it was a basic hostility working its way out through the soles of his feet. One day I came into a room in which he was changing his socks, and read him a stuffy curtain lecture about how unnecessary it was to smell that bad, and dropped the socks out of the window. When I had quite finished, he said: 'That was the clean pair', and I had to go down to the street to get them.

Of course the theory is that every mortal smell can now be got out of a bottle – there's a 'new car smell' for old Fords, you can damp down the cats by rushing at them with a can of Haze, and the scent industry goes on with its priestlike task of reodorizing mankind. But the range is far too narrow. Men's scents may be advertised by lighthouses or gundogs, but they're the same old eau-de-cologne, not the real male smells of petrol and newspaper and mud; girls are only supposed to smell of flowers or sex, though it's male animals it comes from. (I can never understand how they found out about musk in the first place – can you imagine an ideas conference in a scent firm with someone saying: 'Supposing we went to Central Asia and found a deer, there might be a gland up its backside . . .'?)

I think we must now increase the artificial smells to infinity. Spray your woman with 'new wife smell' as an alternative to adultery; if nothing turns you on except fish and chips, get your man to put that behind his ears; fill the kitchen with the smell of tomato sauce, and the children might even eat trout and asparagus and beef. As the girl said about contraception in *Cold Comfort Farm*, 'Tis wicked! Tis flying in the face of Nature! Still, it might be worth trying.'

46 · You Say What You Mean

People have an uncanny habit of meaning what they say –
and of meaning it more often than they notice. A man who
says something as simple as 'Be reasonable, darling,' implies
a belief in sorting things out on a rational basis, rather than
appealing to tradition or natural law. The cop who says 'I'm
only doing my job' has accepted the professional obligation
as more pressing than the personal; a singer sighing, 'Man,
it's wild,' is unconsciously expressing a whole range of convictions about the dead hand of civilization and the vital
spontaneous forces on the jungle border.

Sometimes, of course, the pub philosopher knows that he
is generalizing. 'You can't make an omelette without breaking eggs,' says the union leader who calls a ruinous strike – and
behind him is a whole revolutionary thesis about the end
justifying the means. The woman who casts her eyes upwards
and says 'These things are sent to try us,' is consciously hoping
that someone will note her trials on the credit side of the ledger.

But more often it's instinctive: we have our say, hardly
noticing that the things we are sure of are peculiar to us, to
our own time, to this continent and this society. 'It's not his
mother she's marrying, after all,' we say, forgetting that over
half the globe the girl is almost doing just that. 'I've got a
right to a bit of happiness', sobs the wife who is caught under
the milk-cart, gulping out an expectation about life that
gloomy souls like cavemen and monks would never have
accepted for a moment. And the sensible social worker who
says, 'It's no good crying over spilt milk,' is rejecting in a
sentence the entire Christian doctrine of repentance.

Where do we get our notions from? Teacher or parent,

187

TV or pop star, from a book or a gossip? It doesn't greatly matter; since the teacher read a book, the pop star had parents, even real people sometimes write for TV. Ideas leak down from one person to the next, from generation to generation, and tracing them back may seem as hopeless as trying to work out where you caught your cold. Yet a surprising number are traceable – and to sources as unlikely as the Black Hand in Outer Mongolia, who turns out to be behind the drug smuggling in a thriller.

Take, for example, a handful of views about love and fulfilment and individuality. 'A man's got to believe in himself,' you hear someone say. 'You've got to look after Number One.' 'I never asked to fall in love' – but the assumption is that, having done so, my love must be allowed to go the distance. 'My wife doesn't understand me,' implies that understanding is supposed to be important in marriage, not just duty or good cooking, that a wife's claims are weakened if she is failing to come up with this particular class of goods. Or take that most interesting transference of responsibility – 'She didn't have to say yes,' 'But, Mother, I love him,' wails the teenager, and everybody assumes that this is as good a reason as any for marrying the man. 'I'm funny that way,' says the baby bore, confident that to be different is good; 'I want to be respected as a person,' she says, or a man says, 'That job wouldn't suit me.' Every politician, every argument stresses the rights of the individual.

It comes as a surprise to realize, as the psychiatrist Dr Winnicott has pointed out, how modern and local is this idea: the conviction that an individual has claims more important than those of society or of the family. We think of society as being there to help the happiness of countless individuals, rather than individuals being there to contribute to a healthy society; we think about rights, not duties; but it has not always been so.

Thomas Mann said that the great achievement of the nineteenth century was its intense preoccupation with the feelings of the individual, but it didn't even start there. Some of its roots are with Jean-Jacques Rousseau, the local Swiss lad who asserted that the heart was more important than the head (or at any rate, in his case, more in evidence); but more come from the improbable figure of Kant, walking to the Königsberg docks daily with such precision that they set their clocks by him: there he goes, maintaining that people must be used as ends in themselves and not means; this dry old stick giving an unlikely jet thrust to the entire romantic movement.

For if people are ends in themselves, you can't marry them off to suit the breeding plans of the dynasty, you can't use a woman as a *bête à plaisir;* and the boy's determination to go for art and not the army has to be listened to, if not with joy, at least with a decent respect. Non-interference becomes a virtue, family duty suspect; finding out what the individual's real claims are – i.e. sincerity – becomes important for its own sake.

All this meets a parallel stream pouring down from the high crags of religion: from Martin Luther asserting that every man is his own priest, that no set-up can save your soul for you; from the eighteenth-century evangelical movement that reckoned you had to feel it *here* – though still at a time when the word 'enthusiasm' referred to idiotic unthought-out enterprises, like building a castle on a landslide, or a marriage on romantic love. (What *doesn't* come into it is the fretworked red herring of courtly love: founded on songs sung by semi-queers a long way under the windows of married ladies, this was essentially a substitute for action, not a cause of it.)

But from this gushes Byron and the 'sensitivity' which made Victorian girls think it gross to be seen eating greedily and the absolute determination to find and express your own personality come what may that is abroad in our own day.

189

You stress individuality, and the first individual that springs to mind is likely to be yourself. And from these to the total freak-out: 'Hippies', said my favourite don sourly, 'have a more respectable intellectual ancestry than they deserve.'

Or consider these. 'He's had a run of bad luck,' 'Lightning never strikes in the same place twice,' 'You can't win 'em all,' 'I'm keeping my fingers crossed,' or 'You can't have it both ways.' People say 'Touch wood' or 'DV' without believing in either the Druids or God. There is a wealth of atavistic superstition buried in some of our most humdrum phrases, and it comes out even more strongly in the little superstitions people make for themselves: like not singing before breakfast because it makes for a bad day, not talking about the man or the job you want because if you talk about it They will hear and somehow make it not happen; or the personal conviction of any one punter that the horses he backs are crippled by the very fact of his backing them.

Logic doesn't come into it, any more than it does with a roulette wheel – which *can* come up red yet again; you *can* win them all and some people seem absolutely designed to be struck by lightning, by disaster, over and over again. It is a subterranean appeal to dark forces, just as a sort of primitive fatalism is reflected in phrases like 'His number's up,' or a muddled belief in the general vengefulness of fate in 'He had it coming'.

Even apart from the straight human nastiness of those who go around passing on bad news with the phrase 'I thought you ought to know,' there is an obscure, age-old idea of propitiation, a conviction that you can somehow buy future happiness with present pain – which Samuel Butler at least brought into the open when he defined moral actions as those in which the pain precedes the pleasure (like long engagements and apprenticeships), immoral ones those in which the pleasure precedes the pain (like seduction and alcohol).

And presumably it is this sort of urge which makes people throw halfpennies even into shallow municipal fountains – but once we get into money we're into a very dense forest indeed. 'Sure, if the money's right,' 'Poor guy, he has to live in Switzerland for tax reasons,' 'Nobody can work without incentives' – there are dozens of phrases which show our relation to money: a relation which it never occurs to us is not one universal to makind. But it isn't. In a good many other societies you miss out on money because you go directly for the things that money is supposed to bring: status, security, power over other people. You get these things by being learned or well-born, by holding the serfs at arrow-point or being known to cure warts; in any society based on agriculture, for instance, money can keep its distance. Sure, there was a miser in every medieval morality play, but he was only one oddity, not a whole way of life.

The translation of everything (even, oddly enough, time, in phrases like 'Don't waste my time' and 'Time is money') into terms of money is partly attributable to capitalism's enemies on the Marxist front: if everything is seen in terms of the class struggle and economics, then it is not so much that money buys status as that the reason for respecting the knights was simply that they were richer. The idea has certainly backwashed towards the capitalists themselves, but in their case the money assumes a magic power of its own. Look at phrases like 'It's no good ignoring market forces,' 'You can't run a country with all this Government intereference,' 'We aren't running a Sunday school' – meaning profit first, better washrooms second. A great deal of this apparently hard-headed empiricism reflects a deep-seated conviction that the sums of capitalism must come out right in the end. This is maybe the mystical descendant of Adam Smith and his Hidden Hand; he thought the processes of commerce were ordained to work out well; so we get the idea that only by each man working for himself, doing what is good for him, will things be done well for mankind in general. What Charles Wilson actually said was, 'What's good for the country is good for General Motors,' but it's not surprising that everyone took it that what was good for General Motors was good for the country, because that is the strong hidden belief of every properly commercial man.

More: he thinks that there is something unnatural about any civic attempts to exercise control of Commerce. Nothing in which the word Nature is used usually stands up to much scrutiny (Professor Whitehead used to say, when anyone used it in his hearing, 'Which of the 130 meanings of that word are you employing?') and it certainly doesn't in this case. Sending 500 tons of perfectly real bananas out to sea because something is written on a piece of paper is hardly natural, if by 'natural' you mean that savages do it; conversely interference by the community – the tribal elders or the top gorilla in the pack – is almost older than man. Yet the conviction remains.

*

What about death? Here we know that people's attitudes have changed. No one now says 'Not lost but gone before' as they report that their baby has gone down the plughole, and though you might hear someone saying, 'It was a merciful release,' they would mean from a long and crippling illness, not from the wearisome condition of humanity. To us, suicide is always a calamity, and you never hear someone say, 'He made a good end'; people are far more likely to explain some wild course of action with the phrase 'You can only live once' or – in this age when the expectation of life is double what it was a century ago – that 'Life's too short' to bother with this or that.

The general doubt about what, if anything, lies beyond the grave makes us feel that deathbed scenes are morbid, that patients mustn't be told they are dying, that 'It doesn't do to brood.' It is assumed that no widow stays faithful to the memory of a dead husband from choice, and even funerals aren't the fun they were. In societies where something, however frightful, was planned for the dear departed you could at least gather round and push the boat out, sing songs and swig something: 'Mother, dear. Mother, may I go to the wake?' implies a Christian society where a wake can be the sort of farewell party it is worth being seduced at; no one ever said, 'Mother, dear Mother, may I go to the crematorium?'

All this goes hand in hand with our conviction that our ancestors aren't what they were. To the Greeks, to the Chinese, ancestors were important; religion resided in them; even in the Middle Ages there was a respect for the past as such, a determination to seek ancient authority for any innovation which had the medieval scholars tied in knots trying to reconcile Virgil with the Virgin and vice versa. (The only modern parallel is those who search Marx or Chairman Mao for the last word, or allege that any new psychological theory was implied in a footnote in Freud.) Other societies have often looked to the past for a Golden Age (as the eighteenth century did) for a lost state of nature where the savage was Noble, for a Garden of Eden, a 'good old days'. We have switched to a faith in the future, however much we have to cross our fingers and squeeze our eyes shut to maintain it; and it is implicit in all the phrases about Not Standing in the Way of Progress, or being Unable to Put the Clock Back, and Moving with the Times.

The students in the Paris riots of 1968, and the man who says, 'We'll never get fewer accidents *until* we get a society that has outgrown aggression,' Henry Ford saying that 'History is Bunk' all imply, with Condorcet in the French Revolution, that you have to abolish history and live as if life had just begun (he implied it, that is, till the revolution abolished him). To some extent the young have always wanted to start today as if there hadn't been any yesterday (for one thing, it would let them off the sweat of learning about yesterday); but they are a lot more open now about despising the mess their parents have made of things, and their elders take them much more seriously than they did; and this for a variety of reasons.

'You mustn't *teach* a child to draw!' 'Education is a drawing out not a putting in,' 'I'm only helping him to realize his own potential,' 'We force children to conform to our adult patterns' – all this somehow has a vaguely familiar ring: the ring of what we learnt at school when *we* were being forced into adult patterns, which as like as not included Wordsworth. We all know the feeling of looking at a small child and wondering what the hell is going on in its head; but Wordsworth was convinced that what was going on was divine; that 'not in utter nakedness, But trailing clouds of glory do we come'. He didn't invent it however – nor even did Shelley' who talked of 'the world's slow stain'. Traherne remembered the golden perception of childhood and the whole thing (given of course a helpful push by the Christ Child) probably started with Plato. His theory, you will remember, was that there was an ideal world of which this is but a poor reflection; children had come from it but recently, and remembered still an inkling of the divine.

It is a tribute to the power of the human mind to contain contradictory convictions that those, in education particularly, who are most lovingly attached to the theory of children's essential rightness are often those who also hold most strongly to the power of the environment; which springs from a totally opposite intellectual notion. 'I want him to have the chances I missed.' 'Gee, Officer Krupke, it's just our bringing upke . . . we're depraved because we're deprived!' 'I can't understand it – he's always had the best of everything' – these are the phrases which suggest that the newborn child is a piece of blank paper on which things get written – an idea which started with Locke. The eighteenth-century enlightenment was sure that in order to have the best possible mind a child must receive only the best possible impressions; and from this could be said to spring the whole idea of the deprived child, of a bad family as a factor in delinquency, the vital need for all children to be given equal chances in education since they all start square at birth.

'We hold these truths to be self-evident,' said Thomas Jefferson, 'that all men are created equal . . .' and today people (who don't mean it in the least) feel obliged to say that many of their best friends are coloured. The idea that we start level is compulsory; and it probably wouldn't be if it hadn't originally been for Locke.

The importance of the environment seems to us so self-evident that we find it hard to remember anyone ever believed differently. We forget about royal blood and the idea of hereditary murder; the idea of noble birth has gone under to noble upbringing, blue genes submerged by blue jeans.

But not all systems have always seen it that way. We assume that social engineering is respectable as well as possible, pulling down slums to discourage crime as we drain swamps to discourage mosquitoes. But a Hindu would see this as futile, since he has been cast into a vile situation as a result of misdeeds in another life; many earlier Christians would have regarded it as irrelevant, since anything can be raw material for improving the soul, the only thing that matters – which is the real meaning of the phrase 'All things work together for the best to them that love God'.

It is not just that other societies have been notably bad at alleviating suffering; they haven't been bothering about it anyway. Everybody knows that happiness is pleasant; but it is a Western and recent conviction that happiness is good for you. There's certainly an opposite view, even now. 'Hard work

195

never hurt anyone.' 'They've got it soft, in the South,' 'He can't have everything his own way,' 'When I was your age, I was up at six scrubbing floors' – all express a belief in the metallic view of human life: that one is forged in the furnace, purified by suffering, made tougher and therefore better by adversity. You'd find a lot of this in early religion, and not just in the penances of priests either: not for nothing is the Quaker top brass officially called the Meeting for Sufferings.

No doubt much of it came with the idea of original sin, but has been neatly grafted on to our new environmental concern: 'Give me the child till he is seven,' say the Jesuits; or 'As the twig is bent, so shall the tree grow.' You get two sets of environmentalists, you might say: one better at giving the tree fertilizer and sunshine, the other more interested in pruning and disbudding.

*

Happiness is good for you – and now even pleasure is respectable; we even take it for granted that the two go together. 'A little of what you fancy does you good,' 'A fun thing,' 'Whatever the pleasure, Player's completes it' – the appeal is straightforward enough. Hobbes, writing that deeply melancholy work 'Leviathan' in 1651, had it that all human decisions were based on an attraction to pleasure, a sheering away from pain; the pleasure could be complicated, of course, like going through an ordeal to win the pleasure of approval – or, presumably, slogging away writing 'Leviathan'.

The next two to exalt happiness were not exactly cheerful either: Bentham and Mill with their Utilitarianism: the theory that a State should be run for the greatest possible happiness of the greatest possible number. I suppose we'd mostly take that for granted now; but it's a very different notion from La Gloire or the Third Reich, certainly from any state involving slaves, whether actually called that or not;

and from the medieval scene where one was slotted into place by God and supposed to stick it whether one liked it or not.

And from that sort of concern with civic happiness to Freud: 'We grow on pleasure,' he said – though I'm not saying a man who wrote a book called *Beyond the Pleasure Principle* exactly left it at that. But his theories are certainly taken as giving pleasure an imperative force: every model girl talks about what a mistake it is to be frustrated, inhibitions cause the good housewife as much concern as germs in the S-bend, and we are positively encouraged to follow the devices and desires of our own parts.

This presumption is what Ronald Bryden was inspired to call the hydraulic view of sex: the one that implies you have a given quantity of drive pouring about in your pipes and boilers and it has to go *somewhere*; as opposed to earlier views which treated the thing more like a muscle or a skill, which would be developed by exercise and deline with disuse. (Even as late as the last war a lot of soldiers genuinely though they would risk impotence if they stayed girl-less in the desert too long.)

The old theories don't quite die, the new theories come and change; we base the most profound decisions of our lives on something learnt at a bus-conductor's knee twenty years ago, and no voice ever warns, 'Put down that theory, you don't know where it's been.' The threads of thinking twist and cross and repeat one another; die out or change without anyone noticing; no one stops to think what fiery theory, now maybe quite discredited, started our train on its way. And it's anyone's guess whether the thinkers, even when you find them, actually started their own ideas; or simply expressed what people were beginning to think; or got their name on the theory merely by being slightly ahead of the field. But, as Marcus Aurelius said: 'Nothing comes of Nothing,' and even our most bastard thoughts have parents in the past.

47 · *Goodbye to Bed*

I don't mean what you mean, for a start: this here is a family show. Anyway, it's absurd that 'bed' should mean what you mean, when you think how much else goes on there (quite apart from how much of the other goes on elsewhere: as many good Christians outside the Church as in it, that's what I always say). But they're pulling the old bed down (*boo!*) though they're building another (*hurrah!*). It was a good bed. It was almost a way of life; it shall not pass without a word.

We never had quite such trouble buying it as the excruciated W. B. Yeats, discussing the width with a virgin bride where every three inches put the price up. But at the Bedding Centre we were told by a man who looked like a P. G. Wodehouse butler that if we chose a cheap bed we would 'experience a tendency to roll together towards the centre'. We said we supposed we would anyway, blushed and left abruptly. When we came back from honeymoon the bed was almost the only furniture we had; for years there was nowhere else to sit; so everything came back to it.

Especially cats. In the early days of marriage before I got the upper hand – of the cats, I mean – one used actually to sleep with us. A furred cobra might just possibly have been nastier than that cat Kilroy, snaking his way up my nightdress into my husband's arms, but not much (Kilroy was *where?*). Not that all cats are bad in bed: some pass out solid for fourteen hours. But too many wake in the false dawn, ask themselves 'Is there a God?' and need reassurance. When my husband was sleeping with a Bowie knife under the pillow because the locks weren't on the new doors yet, he more than once felt a pressure on his chest and leapt up armed to the teeth – only to find himself gazing into the face of a fat cat troubled by Doubt.

Kittens rapidly realize that the one place they can't be got at is under the bed – under the exact middle of the bed. We couldn't go to sleep on top lest we crush them to death, so we spent hours with a sardine and a soft broom trying to get them out, while they roosted in the springs, spitting, and their blasted mother wove up and down saying, 'I told you no good would come of it!'

Whatever the chore – letters, hemming curtains, doing the Christmas cards – we could always kid ourselves we were letting ourselves off lightly by doing them in bed; we became expert at sliding in underneath the packing or the tax forms, regardless. The pouch at the bottom where the hot bottles hide – perfect repository for stolen goods – became the obvious place to look for things; and we perfected the fifty-eighth position of love, which is the one adopted to get the hot bottle behind the knees of one and the back of the other and possibly the one known only to the Emperor of China.

Twice I was sent to bed in perfect health for preventive reasons and made the sinister discovery that after five days you're as weak as a leek just from lying there. In that bed I knitted the gnarled grey baby-garment without which no mother thinks she will be safely delivered, and we gave the baby its ten o'clock feed – or rather the two cursory swigs it took before going into its song and dance act. No one actually died or was born in bed, unless you count a litter of kittens delivered on to my husband's feet at six in the morning when I was in hospital having a miscarriage. (He says it's the only time he's had a brandy at 6 a.m. Surely it should have gone to the cat?) Once we had people to dinner and half of them sat on the bed; and more than once it was the scene of poker – not strip poker, but a serious game designed to determine who got up to shut the window.